Pure Evil

Pure Evil

How Tracie Andrews murdered my son, deceived the nation
and sentenced me to a life of pain and misery

MAUREEN HARVEY

JOHN BLAKE

Published by John Blake Publishing Ltd,
3 Bramber Court, 2 Bramber Road,
London W14 9PB, England

www.blake.co.uk

First published in hardback in 2007

ISBN: 978 1 84454 380 9

British Library Cataloguing-in-Publication Data:

A catalogue record for this book is available from the British Library.

Design by www.envydesign.co.uk

Printed in Great Britain by William Clowes Ltd, Beccles, Suffolk

1 3 5 7 9 10 8 6 4 2

Pictures on pages 4, 5 and 6 of the picture section reproduced by kind
permission of News Team International. All other photographs are from
the author's personal collection.

Papers used by John Blake Publishing are natural, recyclable
products made from wood grown in sustainable forests.
The manufacturing processes conform to the environmental
regulations of the country of origin.

Dedication
For my son Lee…

Lee, your life was cut short. I now know why you were always in a hurry. Watching the clock, wearing out the carpet walking up and down the lounge, waiting for your friends to arrive, complaining they were late, ready for a good night on the town.

You lived life to the full and I was so proud of you.

Lee, thank you for being my son and my friend. My love for you will never end.

God bless, my darling. Love you, miss you,
Mum x

Special thanks to Ray, Michelle, Steve, my family, my friend Joyce and to West Mercia Constabulary.

Contents

1

The Nightmare Begins

It was 3.20am on Sunday, 1 December 1996. The sound of a car pulling up outside had woken Ray and me. Who else would turn up in the middle of the night but Lee?

I lay awake in the darkness wondering why I couldn't hear him letting himself in downstairs. Typical, I thought, getting out of bed. He's probably forgotten his front-door key. But, when I pulled back the curtains and saw a white car parked at the end of our drive, I realised it wasn't Lee's. I was horrified when I saw two uniformed police officers get out of the car and make their way up the garden path.

I can remember shouting, 'No!' as they were knocking on the front door and, in that split-second, as Ray leaped out of bed and nearly fell over as he tried to put both legs in one trouser hole, a thousand thoughts raced through my mind. Had Lee been in an accident? Was he hurt? Was it Michelle, my daughter? She was pregnant and on a Center

Parcs holiday with her husband Steve and two-year-old daughter Paige. What in God's name had happened?

Even as Ray and I were running down the stairs, I was silently praying, 'Please, God, let everything be all right. Let them have the wrong address.'

Facing a policeman and woman on the doorstep, I gripped Ray's arm. 'Are you the parents of Lee Harvey?' one of them asked.

The blood was pounding in my head as Ray nodded and stepped back to let them into the hallway.

'I'm afraid he's been in some sort of row,' the officer continued. 'A road-rage attack. He's been stabbed.'

I could hardly breathe. 'Is he all right?' I asked.

His face said it all. 'We're very sorry, Mrs Harvey...'

'Oh, God!' I screamed. 'Please don't tell me he's dead.'

Ray was crying as the officers followed us into the sitting room. The policewoman put her arm round me and said she'd make us a cup of tea. I went into the kitchen and started getting cups out of the cupboard. I was in such a state of shock that I couldn't find anything else. I stood shaking by the sink and let the policewoman gently take a cup from my hands.

This couldn't be happening to us. It happened on the television to other people. I'd read harrowing interviews in the newspapers and magazines where other parents had relived this nightmare. It was too much to take in that now it was our turn and that our son was dead.

'It can't be Lee,' Ray said. His voice was choked, barely audible.

'No,' I heard myself say. 'You've made a mistake... It's not him... It can't be.'

2

'I'm afraid it is Lee,' the first policeman began.

'What about Tracie?' I interrupted him. My mind was racing. Lee stabbed? Murdered? A road-rage attack?

'Was she with him?' I asked. 'Is she hurt?'

'She's been taken to the Alexandra Hospital in Redditch,' he said, watching Ray pace up and down the room. 'She's in shock and has some bruising from where she was attacked, but she's all right. We'll be talking to her later.'

'What do you mean, "She's all right"?' Ray demanded. 'Why didn't she phone us? If she was with Lee when someone killed him, she's a witness. Why would anyone leave a witness to identify them?'

Even when you're facing the kind of shock that feels like a sledgehammer punch in the chest, like someone is squeezing the breath out of you, you still, somehow, focus on trying to make sense of the unthinkable.

Tracie Andrews... we'd lost count of the times our son had driven or caught a taxi back home in the early hours after yet another row with Tracie. The arguments between them were the only predictable thing about their on-off relationship.

Usually, after one or both of them had downed one too many drinks, Tracie would end up either phoning her mum or the police to say she wanted Lee out of her flat for good. She'd claim he was throwing things at her, threatening her, taunting her. Like us, the police knew it was a case of six of one and half-a-dozen of the other and would log the call as another domestic. They'd turn up, Tracie would turn on the waterworks and play the victim, and Lee would pick up his jacket and leave. He'd get home covered in scratches and

3

bruises, while Tracie would be crying on her mum's shoulder, blaming Lee for causing yet another bust-up.

A couple of days later, the phone would ring and Lee would listen to her in floods of tears begging him to come back... and off he'd go. That was just the way things were between them. Tracie seemed to thrive on the drama and Lee was so besotted with her that, for most of the two years they'd been together, he wouldn't have a bad word said against her. Just so long as they ended up in bed together once they'd kissed and made up, he went along with it.

Ray and I had given up trying to convince him that they'd never be happy together, even though they were engaged and planning their wedding. Arrogant and self-obsessed, Tracie had been bad news from the day we'd met her. We'd both recognised a controlling young woman whose bleached blonde hair and caked-on make-up masked a deep insecurity and manipulative personality. She was the kind of good-time girl who ruthlessly traded on her sexuality to seek the attention she craved.

Lee, a good-looking lad, who'd bedded more women than he'd had hot dinners, saw what every other red-blooded male would have seen – another trophy girlfriend who wouldn't take much persuading to get into bed.

'He's not in love,' Ray had said to me when Lee brought Tracie home for Sunday lunch a week after they'd met in Baker's nightclub in Birmingham. 'He's in lust.'

That had been back in May 1994. We'd all hoped we'd see the back of her within a few weeks and that Lee would see through her. But sex was always Tracie's trump card and, within just six months of meeting Lee, she had a diamond engagement ring on her finger and was planning a full-on white wedding to prove it.

'We're meant to be together,' she'd announced on the day Lee brought her home to meet us. 'It's our destiny.'

Lee could have had his pick of any girl who caught his eye. But Tracie was different, he'd told me. 'It's the best sex I've ever had, Mum,' he'd joked.

There was nothing he and I didn't talk about and I was used to hearing him describe how he'd often get home from work and find her waiting for him in stockings and suspenders, ready to drag him upstairs. Lee had even told Michelle, his sister, that he thought he'd tried most things in bed until he met Tracie.

But even knowing how besotted Lee was with her wasn't enough for Tracie. From the moment they'd met, she'd tried every trick in the book to drive a wedge between him and us. She carried a deep-rooted insecurity that made her cynical and paranoid. Everyone, or so she thought, was trying to take Lee away from her. Tracie was especially jealous of his relationship with his five-year-old daughter Danielle's mum Anita Curtis and the fact that Lee was so close to his sister.

It was far from ideal, and particularly heart-breaking for me because we were so close and I couldn't bear to see him so unhappy when he'd turn up at home after yet another argument. You never stop worrying about your kids or wanting to protect them, no matter what age they are, but as adults they have to lead their own lives, and learn from their own mistakes. It's hard to sit on the sidelines and watch, but it's part and parcel of being a parent. If you get too involved, it can make things worse. Once you've said your piece, you just have to let them get on with it.

In the week leading up to 1 December, I hadn't seen Lee for a week. He'd moved back in with Tracie three months before, even though we'd told him, yet again, that he was making a big mistake. But then they'd had another huge bust-up and Lee had come home yet again.

'If you even think about going back to her again after all this crap, you needn't bother coming back here again,' Ray had shouted when Lee said he was going to try to sort things out with her once and for all. 'We're not running a bloody hotel, you know.'

I followed Lee into the kitchen and watched him slam a half-drunk coffee on the sink unit.

'Jean will let me stay with her,' Lee said angrily. 'She won't mind having me.'

Lee had stayed with Ray's sister before when Ray had told him he was sick of him leaving Tracie and then coming home with his tail between his legs. But, on this occasion, Ray was having none of it. 'Oh, no, you're not going to Jean's,' he shouted. 'You're not involving my family in this nightmare with that little slut.'

I didn't want to take sides because, like Ray, I'd had enough of Tracie getting her own way. It seemed like she only had to snap her fingers and Lee would cave in and go running back to her. I knew Ray was only trying to make a point but at the same time I couldn't bear the thought of Lee having nowhere to go.

'Oh, for God's sake, Ray,' I said, 'this is his home. He can come back any time he likes.'

Lee had said nothing as he picked up his car keys and walked towards the front door.

'You're making the biggest mistake of your life, son,' Ray shouted. 'She's not worth all the grief she gives you.'

'Right! I'll go and live in a hostel,' said Lee. 'At least I'll get some bloody peace and quiet.'

I knew Ray was trying to get Lee to change his mind and that he was just as angry and frustrated as I was. We all say things we regret in the heat of the moment. Especially when you love someone and don't want to see them hurt. But I know, even after all this time, that the memory of that afternoon is one that will haunt Ray until he takes his last breath. Not just because of what he'd said to Lee, but because he let him walk out without saying goodbye.

Normally – but then nothing was normal after Tracie Andrews came into our lives – they'd have been hugging each other, joking, enjoying the lad–dad banter that was so much a part of their relationship. They adored each other but they were both pig-headed, stubborn men.

Lee had left the house after saying goodbye to me, Michelle and her husband Steve but had barely given his dad a second glance. He knew how angry and disappointed Ray was but he also knew that neither of them was prepared to back down.

I was so relieved when Lee turned up a few days later. 'Where have you been staying?' I asked him.

'Mum, I'm fine,' he said, 'don't worry about me... I've just come back to get some more clothes. I'm back at Tracie's. She's not as bad as you think she is and I love her, Mum. We really are going to make it work this time. OK?'

7

I looked at him. He was grinning. I loved him so much it was impossible to stay cross with him. There was nothing I could say or do to stop him being with Tracie. I shrugged my shoulders. 'OK, it's your life,' I said.

That night in December, it wouldn't have mattered if Lee had come home and woken us up. We'd missed him so much and I knew Ray would be really chuffed. I knew he'd regretted losing his temper. He'd even taped an American football game for Lee that evening so I knew how much he was missing him.

And, anyway, the house wasn't the same without Lee around. He livened things up with his crap jokes and funny stories. The music on his stereo was always playing too loudly, the washing machine was always full of his clothes and the frying pan was always sizzling with eggs and bacon. In fact, he'd often come home late after a night out with the boys and ask me to make him bacon, egg and chips. It didn't matter how late it was, or whether I was engrossed in a film or something on the television, I'd happily start cooking. Ray knew that, if he had asked for a cup of tea after 8pm, he wouldn't have stood a chance. The kitchen was closed to everyone – except Lee.

Sometimes, Ray would be upstairs in bed and would hear our laughter and the clatter of pans; or the smell of bacon, egg and chips cooking would waft upstairs and he'd come down to the kitchen. 'I don't believe it!' he'd say, just like the character from *One Foot in the Grave*. Lee even nicknamed his Dad 'Victor Meldrew' after that!

Lee loved to laugh and chat and I loved to sit with him, listening to his jokes and his stories about the night out he'd just had. He would make me laugh so much that Ray would often bang on the bedroom floor and yell, 'Oi, you two – some of us have to get up early, you know.'

Now, I miss the laughter and our late-night suppers more than anything.

Like us, his mates had got used to the on-off situation with Tracie, and the moment they knew he was living back home, they hardly left him alone. Every evening, a crowd of lads would turn up ready to hit the town. Lee loved it. But only because he always knew it would be only a matter of time before it was all hearts and flowers again with Tracie.

I instantly knew Ray suspected Tracie must have had something to do with Lee's death, even though he never said anything while the police were there.

At that stage, neither of us wanted to believe Lee was dead. The police had told us that she'd been attacked as well, so how could she have been involved? She might have been the last woman in the world I'd wanted Lee to end up with but, for all her faults, I was convinced she loved him.

I can remember sitting on the sofa in our living room, shaking so much that when the policewoman handed me a cup of tea, I spilled it down my nightie. It was scalding hot but I hardly felt a thing as I looked at Ray sitting next to me with his head in his hands.

The policewoman asked if we could phone someone to sit with us. A neighbour or a friend perhaps?

'We've got a lot of information coming in already,' the policeman said. 'We'll be able to tell you a lot more as soon as we hear. I think you need someone with you.'

I shook my head. We'd lived in our house for 20 years,

going out to work, bringing up our children, never causing anyone any problems or bothering them. The only person I knew I wanted to speak to was my brother Alan. We were from a family of nine children and he and I had always been close. Four years earlier, he'd lost his only son Spencer in a terrible road accident. It had happened the day before his 17th birthday. Cycling to his job at Next, he'd been knocked off his bike by a lorry and had died when he got to hospital.

He and Lee had grown up together and had been very close. He was such a lovely lad and had started training to be a fireman when he died. It had always been his dream job but, as he had to wait until his 18th birthday to join the Fire Service, his job at Next had been a stop-gap. Alan had been through this nightmare. He'd know what to do, what to say.

Alan's daughter answered the phone and passed it over to her dad when I asked to speak to him.

'I know how you feel about losing Spencer,' I blurted out when Alan asked me what was wrong.

'Lee's been in a road-rage attack. Oh, God, Alan, he's been murdered. Can you come over?'

Alan didn't ask me any questions. He said he was on his way and rang off.

I told the police I didn't want them to contact Michelle. She was 27 at the time, two years older than Lee, and they'd always been so close. I couldn't begin to imagine how she'd take in any of this. The thought that she might hear about it on the news was unthinkable. I just wanted her to get home safely with Steve and Paige before Ray and I got to her and told her what had happened.

The officers looked at each other. 'We can tell them for you,' the policeman said.

Ray was on his feet, still crying.

'No,' I shouted. 'Ray and I will deal with it. She's pregnant.'

The policeman nodded. 'Don't worry, we'll keep Lee's name from the press until then,' he said.

Alan and his wife Babs arrived within ten minutes of my call. Their journey from Sheldon in Birmingham would normally have taken a good half-an-hour but Alan later told me he'd driven at 90mph most of the way.

Ray and I were in tears again as soon as they came through the front door. I can remember all of us hugging each other and crying as we explained what the police had told us.

'None of this rings true,' Alan said quietly, as he held me in his arms. 'Why didn't Tracie phone you?'

The policeman shook his head. 'We don't know any more than what we've told you,' he said. 'There's bound to be a lot more information coming in to the incident team and, as soon as they know more, you'll be told.'

'I want to see Lee,' I told the officers. 'You could have made a mistake, but, if it really is him, then I need to be with him. I'm going now.'

The police explained that Cooper's Hill, the lane where it had happened in Alvechurch, just three miles from our home in King's Norton, would be closed to enable officers from the West Mercia Police Forensics Team to begin their investigation into Lee's death. 'No one but the police will be allowed there,' the policeman said.

I was crying again. 'Please,' I begged him. 'Please let us see Lee.'

The policeman took out his phone and punched in a number. He walked into the kitchen as he spoke. I could hear him telling whoever he was speaking to that we were devastated. I looked at Ray, the tears rolling down my face as he came back into the sitting room moments later.

Alan was trying to calm me down. 'They've got to get as much evidence as possible,' he said gently. 'You can't just go charging up there.'

I knew he was right but all I kept seeing in my mind was Lee lying in the road alone.

The policeman came back into the room. 'I'm afraid it's just not possible, Maureen,' he said. 'You'll be able to see him as soon the forensics team has finished its work.'

'Couldn't I speak to whoever you've just spoken to?' I pleaded. 'They must be able to tell us something else.'

The policeman handed me the phone.

'Mrs Harvey?' I heard a calm voice on the end of the line. 'I'm so sorry but this is a murder inquiry and it's vital that we get all the evidence. We've set up a roadblock to stop anyone going up the lane...'

'I just want to be with Lee,' I interrupted him. 'I'm his mum.'

The incident officer waited for me to finish. 'I don't know if this helps in any way, but Lee wouldn't have felt any pain. He sustained multiple stab wounds and lost a lot of blood. He would have gone very quickly.'

Whoever spoke to me that night did the best job anyone could have done under the horrifying circumstances to calm me down and bring me to my senses. However painful it was to listen to, I knew what he was saying was right and handed the phone back to the policeman.

'Have you phoned Anita yet?' Alan asked.

I looked at Ray and shook my head. Lee had split up with Anita three years earlier but they'd remained close friends because of their little girl Danielle and the fact Lee had wanted her to be a big part of his life and ours. I can still remember Lee sitting on the edge of my bed the night he came home and told me Anita was pregnant. 'It wasn't planned, Mum,' he admitted. 'But I know I can be a good dad.'

He was only 20 at the time and money was tight, but Ray and I knew his child would never be short of love. When Lee split up with Anita two years later, he remained devoted to Danielle. He moved back home and set about converting our spare room for her. When she came to stay at the weekends, she'd spend hours setting up furniture in the doll's house he'd bought and repainted for her.

Lee was the best dad any little girl could have wished for – caring, kind, generous and loving. He would push Danielle on the swing, sit on the seesaw and jump on the trampoline with her. Like so many little girls, she was mad about prams and pushchairs and Lee would take her for a walk so that she could take her dollies out in the pram. He'd let her help him wash his car and then they would get a little bucket and sponge so that she could wash her bike too. He would always sing songs with her, watch videos and pretend to be the customer in her game of shops. He never tired of drinking the endless cups of pretend tea that she made for him in her wendy house.

One time, he and Michelle took Danielle to feed the ducks. There weren't many ducks at the pond, but, as soon as Lee started to throw bread, hundreds of ducks, geese and God knows what else appeared from nowhere and completely surrounded the three of them. When they started pecking him, Lee had to pick Danielle up and they all made a run for it!

We never saw Lee happier than when he was with his girl. Like two peas in a pod. They had the same brown eyes and dark hair and absolutely adored each other.

Tracie's daughter Carla, from a previous relationship, was only a year older than Danielle and the two girls had always got on well. It had been one of so few positive things about her time with Lee. The fact that they both had children had always meant that, when they weren't arguing, at least they could share the happiness of being parents to two happy, healthy little girls.

The thought of Anita finding out about Lee through a radio or TV bulletin was unbearable and, although I had no idea what I was going to say as I dialled her number, I knew I had to find the words.

'Anita, it's Maureen...' I said, when she answered the phone. 'I'm sorry to ring you at this time but Lee's been involved in a road-rage incident.'

I could hear the panic rising in her voice as she asked me if he was all right.

'Anita, listen to me... Lee's been murdered.' My voice was breaking as the words came out. 'I'm so sorry to be telling you on the phone but I had to let you know before someone came and knocked on your door or you heard it on the news.'

I could hear her crying as she asked me what had happened.

'We don't know very much,' I continued, hardly able to believe what I was saying. It was like I was talking about someone else. 'The police have told us he's been stabbed. Tracie's in hospital but she's OK.'

I knew Anita was barely able to take in what I was saying to her. Like us, the shock and disbelief had left her unable to do anything but cry.

'I'll have to tell Danielle later,' she said tearfully. 'I can't believe this is happening.'

'We've all got to be strong for her,' I said. 'I'll let you know as soon as we know more.'

'I know,' she said. 'I'll come over later.'

It must have been about 7.30am when the police left. 'We'll be in touch,' the policeman said. 'I'm sure you'll be able to go and identify Lee today.'

Identify Lee? I think it was then that the penny really dropped. I wasn't going to see Lee. I was going to identify his body.

2

The Reality of Grief

Once Ray, Alan, Babs and I were alone, we agreed Ray and I would get dressed while Alan began phoning the family. I still don't know to this day how Alan managed to keep it all together. He and Babs had already been through so much after losing Spencer and yet they were fantastic.

Ray and I had been there for them then but we hadn't ever imagined the enormity of their pain, how they'd felt, what they'd suffered. I don't think Ray and I will ever be able to thank them for the love and support they gave us in those first devastating hours. We'd never have coped without them.

We were in such a state that I don't think it would have occurred to us that we'd need to start letting everyone know in our family. Apart from Michelle and Steve and Alan and Babs, the only person we wanted to speak to was Tracie.

As far as we were concerned, she had all the answers.

'Well, we just can't sit here drinking bloody tea,' I told Babs. 'I'm going to try and get hold of Tracie.'

There was no answer from her flat so I phoned her mum Irene's house. Tracie's stepdad Alan Carter, Irene's second husband, picked up the phone.

'She's too upset to speak to anyone, Maureen,' he told me when I asked if I could talk to her. 'And she's tired, she's had no sleep. The police took her from the hospital at one o'clock this morning to Redditch Police Station to make a statement. Can you ring back later?'

I could feel the anger rising. 'Why didn't she ring us from the hospital, Alan?'

There was a silence. 'She couldn't remember your number,' he replied. 'Ring back later.'

When I told Ray, Alan and Babs what he'd said, Ray exploded. We'd sat up all night waiting for answers and all Alan could tell us was that she was upset.

'What does he mean, she couldn't remember our bloody number?' spat Ray. 'She's never had any trouble remembering it before.'

Ray was right. Every time Tracie and Lee had a row and split up, she'd be on the phone asking to speak to him within hours. It didn't matter how many times we told her that Lee was out or that he didn't want to talk to her, she'd still keep phoning, screaming down the phone that she knew he was there.

However far-fetched her excuse about not contacting us seemed, I was still determined to defend Tracie. 'Maybe the police wanted to tell us,' I suggested. 'If they've been questioning her, she probably didn't get the chance to phone us, Ray.'

I was too upset and exhausted to listen to him putting two and two together and getting five when none of us knew the facts. Besides which, Ray had drunk three or four large brandies by then, a drink he never normally touched, and was so distraught that I knew it was pointless to offer any rational suggestions about why she hadn't phoned.

Staring back at my reflection in the bathroom mirror as I splashed water on my face and cleaned my teeth, things made even less sense. With so many unanswered questions whirling around in my head and the thought of how I'd break the news to Michelle, I felt completely lost and utterly confused. It seemed like a lifetime ago since Ray and I had almost fallen down the stairs to open the front door and yet, as I went into the bedroom to change out of my nightie, it seemed like it had only just happened.

I put on the jeans and top I'd been wearing the night before, raked my fingers through my hair and went downstairs. As Ray went to change, I rang the police. Whatever they were going to tell me, I'd decided I wasn't going to take no for an answer. I didn't care how long I had to wait around in some police station, I had to see Lee. They told me they were planning to bring Tracie back to the police station for further questioning but that we could come to the hospital and identify Lee's body.

Only a parent who has gone through the overwhelming pain and anguish of having to look at the lifeless body of their child will understand how Ray and I felt that day. It is the most devastating and unbearable ordeal that a human being can ever face. Something that, as a mum or dad, you never imagine having to go through. Shocking, numbing, heartbreaking.

Anyone whose child has been murdered knows that a light goes out from the moment you are told, but the sickening sense of loss and overwhelming sorrow comes with the actual moment you see them. Whatever fragile hope you may have held on to, any flicker of hope that it just might not be your child disappears as you stand in the mortuary and realise that they are never coming back. That you are never again going to see their smile, hear their voice, their laughter.

The police had again told us that Lee had sustained a number of knife wounds so we had no idea what to expect. Ray was shaking so much he could hardly walk as we went into the mortuary with Alan and our police liaison officer DS Mick O'Donnell. Not knowing what to expect when we saw Lee was obviously affecting him badly, whereas I just wanted to hold our son in my arms.

Within a few minutes of getting into the room, Ray was in such a terrible state that he had to leave. I thought he was going to collapse as I watched him stroke Lee's face. 'I'm sorry, I can't cope,' he said, rushing to the door.

I was crying as I heard Ray retching and sobbing outside in the corridor. It's a memory I will never be able to forget, like the image of pain in Alan's face as he stood next to me and Babs gazing at Lee.

I looked at my beautiful boy as the tears rolled down my face, hardly able to comprehend how perfect he looked. Apart from three plasters on his face, on his forehead, cheek and chin, there was no sign of the brutality that had ended his life, no blood, no bruising. He looked as though he was asleep.

I kissed him gently all over his face and stroked his cheek and hair. I couldn't believe how cold he was. Cold and still. 'Don't worry, Lee,' I told him. 'We're going to find who did this to you, Bab.' 'Bab' was what I'd always affectionately called Lee; it's a Brummie term of endearment used for someone close.

Feeling the loss and horror when I looked at him, I thought about the past. When he was only four or five, one of his friends had hit Lee in the face after they had fallen out over something. Ray had seen it happen and had told Lee to hit the boy back, to stand up for himself. But Lee didn't want to and he wouldn't! His dad wanted him to defend himself, but it just wasn't in Lee's nature to be violent; he would shout to get his point across but avoided confrontation.

I lost all sense of time and reality in the moments that I spent with him that first time. It was shocking and, looking back, I don't think I'd have coped as well as I did if I hadn't seen my mum and dad after they died.

Ray's dad had died when he was only eight months old, but, when his mum died of cancer at the age of 63, he didn't want to go and see her. I made him go because I thought he'd regret it. And I'd seen my cousin (my dad's sister Beatrice's son). He'd died, aged 17, with his 16-year-old girlfriend in a motorbike accident and, although I'd been quite young at the time of the funeral, I remembered my dad taking me to my auntie Queen's house to see him in his coffin. I was frightened but Auntie Queen had put her arm around me. 'The dead won't hurt you, Maureen,' she'd said. 'It's nice to kiss their head or their hand. If you kiss them goodbye, they never come back to haunt you.'

Auntie Queen was the psychic in our family. Maybe it was losing her son, but she definitely had what you'd call a second sight. She'd turned around when Lee had only been about three or four and said, 'You've got to watch your boys.'

It was a strange thing to say but I've never forgotten it. There were five boys in our family. Auntie Queen's son Christopher died when he was 17; Alan and Babs had lost Spencer; and Ray's brother and his sister had both lost their sons – Raymond, 20, and Alan, who was only 29.

Now we'd lost Lee. On a Sunday – the same day that all the other boys, except Spencer, had died.

I must have stayed with him that first time for about 15 minutes. The shock was still all-consuming but, after the first few minutes, I felt an extraordinary sense of calm and peace. Of course, I knew he was dead but it didn't stop me wishing, hoping even, that he'd open his eyes and smile at me.

What in God's name was I going to say to Michelle? How I was going to tell her that the brother she loved had been murdered? I just wanted her to come home so that I could hold her in my arms. She'd only married Steve seven months earlier in May 1996 and they were expecting a little brother or sister for Paige. The thought of how suddenly being caught up in this nightmare might affect Michelle's pregnancy was heartbreaking.

The female mortuary attendant was lovely. So kind and calm. She asked me if I was feeling OK.

'I can't stop crying,' I said.

The physical pain of seeing Lee was by now making me clutch my chest and fight to steady my breathing. I felt sick to the stomach. It seemed unreal that I would never see him. Hold him in my arms or breathe in the fragrance of his freshly washed hair. Watch him scoop up Danielle in his arms and swing her round. One of my last memories of Lee had been of him dancing to loud music as he was trying to shave and eat a sandwich at the same time. There never seemed to be enough time in the day for him. Perhaps he'd known he didn't have long in this life.

Lost in grief, images of Lee flashing through my mind, I flinched as the attendant put her arm around me. 'It's natural to cry,' she said. 'Have the police told you anything about his injuries?'

'Just that he'd been stabbed,' I said, unable to take my eyes from Lee's body.

'He has 42 stab wounds,' she said. 'There are about 30 wounds around his neck and chest. And there's one in his back. The small cuts on his fingers would suggest he's tried to defend himself. The fatal wound was the one that severed his carotid artery in his neck. He would have lost a great deal of blood.'

I was shaking from head to toe as I listened to her. Whoever had done this to Lee had used the knife in such a frenzy that he hadn't stood a chance. And, if he'd been stabbed in the back, had he been walking away from whoever had attacked him, not realising perhaps they had a knife?

Still shaking, I nodded when she asked me if I'd like to take a break and let her lead me back into the corridor where Ray was sitting.

'I'm sorry, Maureen,' he sobbed. 'I couldn't stay in there. I just can't do this.'

Sitting next to Ray, I couldn't find the words to tell him that I understood or that it was all right. I just couldn't believe this was happening to us, let alone take in the reality that Lee was lying dead in the next room.

I didn't want to leave the hospital. I just wanted to be with Lee. After a few minutes, I asked if I could go in and see him again on my own.

Back in the mortuary, I touched his face again, still surprised by how cold he felt. And then I lifted up the sheet that was covering him. I wanted to see what had happened to him but he was swathed up to the neck in white bandage. Probably from the post mortem. I couldn't bear the thought that he'd had to go through that. I wanted to hold his hand but placed the sheet gently back over him. I was thinking, You can't go there, he deserves his dignity.

I could have stayed there, just looking at him and talking to him. Looking back, as I so often do, it was probably the closest I'd felt to Lee since being told about his death. The physical pain of just wanting to take him in my arms and breathe the life back into him was overwhelming. Those who have gone through this will know how unbelievably shocking it is to sit with your child who you have known, loved and cared for since the day they were born and try to comprehend the idea that they are never coming back. I think that, no matter how long you sit there, it's never long enough. You just don't want to leave them.

'I can't leave him here alone,' I whispered to the attendant. 'He needs his mum. I love him so much. Please let me stay here with him.'

The attendant nodded and touched my arm. 'Maureen, you can come back and see Lee any time you want to,' she said. 'And you can stay with him as long as you like.'

It was just what I needed to hear. The thought of being able to see him again was enough to help me out of the room and go back to Ray. Alan took over after that. He'd gone through the same grim procedure with his own son. He knew what Ray and I were going through. We couldn't have gone through all the formalities of signing the identification documents without him.

As we left the hospital to go to Michelle's, I was praying she hadn't heard anything about Lee's death on the car radio. She usually listened to nursery rhyme cassettes with Paige, singing along to all the words as they drove along. Please, God, she and Steve had been singing and not listening to the news.

The police had assured us that they wouldn't release any details until we'd had a chance to break the news to her and Steve, but I couldn't rest while there was still an outside chance they'd find out.

I phoned Kim, one of the girls who helped out in the hairdressing salon in King's Heath that Michelle and I owned, and broke the news to her. I couldn't risk Michelle trying to get hold of me there and then worrying because I hadn't turned up for work.

Even though it was a busy time with customers booking appointments to go out to Christmas parties, work was the last thing on my mind.

She was brilliant and said she'd hold the fort and do anything I needed. If Michelle rang, she'd tell her I'd taken the day off.

It was a good move because, when we got to her house, Michelle had already phoned the salon and was wondering where I'd got to. Days off were never on my agenda, especially when she knew how busy we'd be at that time of the year. Seeing me and her dad with Alan and Babs getting out of the car, I knew by the look on her face that she realised something was wrong.

'You don't have to come in with us,' I told Babs as she closed the car door. 'This must be so painful for you after what you've been through with Spencer.

Babs squeezed my arm as I followed Ray up the path. 'It's OK,' she said. 'We're dealing with it.'

Michelle's screams were deafening as I told her about Lee. She stood in her kitchen, banging her fist on the sink unit. 'That fucking bitch did this!' she screamed. 'She's killed Lee!'

Like Ray, Michelle was immediately in no doubt about the identity of Lee's killer. Ray hadn't said Tracie's name but, as he stood crying in Michelle's kitchen, I knew he was thinking the same thing.

'Oh, God, Michelle, don't, please,' I said. I knew she was only saying what Ray had thought from the moment the police had arrived at our house, but I didn't want to believe it. I took Michelle in my arms as Steve tried to

26

comfort Paige, a sobbing little girl unable to understand her mum's grief.

Michelle said that the night before she had suffered a massive panic attack. Sweating profusely and unable to get her breath, she described having experienced severe stabbing pains in her chest and acute breathlessness. It had been so bad she'd had to go outside to get air and Steve had been so worried he'd thought she was having a heart-attack. The astonishing thing for all of us was that it had happened at around 10.30–10.45pm, the time when Lee had taken his last breath.

The hugs and tears never stopped that day. And, even when we took Michelle and Steve back to the hospital to see Lee, the reality of his death still really didn't sink in.

That same afternoon, we visited the police incident room at Redditch Police Station. Mick offered to take us because, even though he couldn't tell us very much, he knew we weren't going to sit at home, drinking endless cups of tea. I've never been the type to take 'no' for an answer and, well, I guess, with me being me, I didn't care what I said or who I said it to. We needed to know anything they could tell us. And, like anyone who's gone through this, you need to feel as though you're doing something.

I'd seen plenty of incident rooms on the telly but had never imagined that I'd end up in one in real life. And never in a million years, in one set up to investigate the murder of my own son.

It was scary because it took us all back to the horror of being told about Lee and because nothing was hidden from us. It was just like the ones you see on *The Bill* – police officers sitting behind computers, desks covered with files and paper, telephones and a huge white board on the wall covered with photos of Lee's body, his car and views of Cooper's Hill. Even the photo I'd given to the policeman and woman who'd told us about Lee's death was pinned up. It was one I'd taken of Tracie and Lee. Ray and I had been for a meal with them at a local pub and I'd decided to capture the moment.

In the days, weeks and months that followed Lee's death, it became a signature photo accompanying reports of his murder.

'All we want is for you to be honest with us,' I told Mick as we left. 'Anything you can tell us, anything at all.'

He nodded. 'Leave it to us,' he said. 'There's more information coming in all the time. You need to go home and try and get some rest if you can. We'll come back with you and help you deal with the media. You and Ray will need to come back and give statements so you can't say anything to any reporters.'

It was a lot easier said than done. When we got back home, the street was full of cars and vans – reporters, photographers and camera crews who had picked up the news of Lee's murder on the West Mercia Police crime log that afternoon were camped outside our house. Like us, they had been given the barest details based on what Tracie had told the police. At that stage, all anyone had to go on was what the police had told us when they'd come to the house: that they had been chased by two men in a car on their way from a pub. And, when Lee stopped his car and got out to challenge them, he'd been attacked and killed by one of them.

Like the police, we knew the media had a job to do and that the coverage of Lee's murder was going to be a vital part of helping with the investigation, but we still weren't prepared for the relentless door-knocking and interview requests that continued throughout the day. Having seen so many fleeting images of distraught, grieving faces in the media over the years, and never really understanding what any of those bereaved relatives were going through, it was now our turn in the spotlight... we now had our own tragic story to tell, and desperately needed whatever help we could get.

3

Suspicion

We saw Tracie for the first time at Redditch Police Station the next day. I broke the silence as Ray and I walked into the interview room where Tracie was sitting at a table. 'Are you OK?' I asked her.

She lifted her head but didn't look at us.

'How long have you been here?' I asked. I was shocked by her appearance. Her hair was matted with blood and her face was swollen. There was a gash above her left eye, which had been taped, and purple bruising beneath her left eye which was spreading across her cheek.

'All night,' she whimpered. 'I went home for an hour and then they brought me back here for more questioning. I don't know why. They just keep asking me loads of questions.'

Ray and I had plenty of questions we wanted to ask her. She was the key to helping the police catch Lee's killers.

'I know it's hard, but the police have to catch the people who did this to Lee,' I told her.

I asked her if she'd been given anything to eat. She shook her head. 'I haven't had anything. I haven't had any sleep.'

What a bloody shame, I thought. I felt genuinely sorry for her. She looked like shit, nothing like the perfectly made-up Tracie we were used to seeing. It was hard to imagine that this was the same person who had spent the best part of two hours in our bathroom putting her face on. Not caring that we'd be waiting to use the loo, crossing our legs outside the door. Seeing Tracie without her slap on just didn't happen, unless you caught her unawares, like the time she'd stayed over at our house and thought no one was about when she tiptoed out of the bedroom clutching her make-up bag.

I'd thought it was hilarious when I came up the stairs and saw her on the landing. But, instead of seeing the funny side, she'd screamed, dashed into the bathroom and slammed the door.

I asked one of three police officers in the room if they could give her a break and some food. 'She's only been home for a wash,' I snapped. 'You could at least get her something to eat.'

When they asked her if she wanted anything, she said she'd like some tea and a sausage sandwich. Ten minutes later, I watched in amazement as she wolfed down the sandwich and drained the mug of tea. Ray and I hadn't managed to eat a thing and yet Tracie couldn't get her sandwich down her neck fast enough.

We were desperate to ask her questions but the police

made it clear they hadn't finished with her. And, when she'd finished her sandwich, they told us we had to leave so they could carry on questioning her.

'We'll see you later, love,' I told Tracie. 'The police need to find out who did this to Lee. It's their job.'

'We need to have a chat with you and Ray,' one of the officers said, as he led us out of the room.

That afternoon, I took Anita to the hospital to see Lee. I knew it would be hard for her but it was something she needed to do. He'd been moved to the little chapel at the hospital. It was beautiful and so much more peaceful and dignified than the mortuary where Ray and I had first seen him. Anita wept as she kissed Lee's face and told him she would never let Danielle forget him. 'I'll tell her how much you loved her,' she whispered. 'And what a good dad you were.'

As she was talking to him, telling him that we'd find out who had done this to him, I thought for a moment that I saw Lee's head move and his eyes flicker. However irrational it sounds, I can only imagine that it's an image many parents can relate to. You know your child has gone and yet you instinctively hang on to the hope that they are going to open their eyes. You know they're not breathing but there's still something very comforting about being with them.

I wept when Anita told me how Danielle had cried when she broke the news of Lee's death. She'd told her that her daddy was in a nice place with Jesus and that he was safe so no one could ever harm him again.

At bedtime, she'd gone into Danielle's room to see if she was asleep and found her gazing out of the window.

'You see that star up there, Mummy?' Danielle had asked her.

Anita knelt next to her and stroked her hair.

'The big bright star shining up there in the sky,' said Danielle. 'Well, that's my daddy's star. I've been standing here looking for Daddy and now I think I've found him.'

Even now, all these years later, the image of Lee's star shining in the darkness is one that Danielle finds comforting. The courage of all children who are forced to try to make sense of losing a parent is one of the most amazing and precious gifts we can ever receive. Anyone who has experienced the gut-wrenching pain of having to tell a child they're not going to see their mummy or daddy, sister or brother again will know how humbling it is to watch them cope with their grief.

At the age of five, Danielle's perfect, innocent, happy world was torn apart and yet her optimism and unshakeable belief in his existence, albeit in another world, helped all of us. While Lee's death forced us, as adults, to question our faith and ask ourselves why, if there was a God, Lee had been taken from us, it was impossible to dismiss Danielle's childish logic. If she could believe in Lee's star, then so could we.

Anita brought her round to see us for an hour that afternoon. However heartbreaking it was to take her in our arms and reassure her that her daddy was in heaven, we knew we had to be strong for her.

One night, just before Christmas, Michelle and I decided to go back to Cooper's Hill. It was where we both felt we

34

could be close to Lee. As we stood together saying prayers at the spot where he'd died, I looked up at the sky and asked him to give us a sign that he was in heaven. Michelle said the same thing out loud and we suddenly saw a shooting star. It was, without doubt, the answer to our prayers that we'd both hoped for.

On Tuesday, 3 December, the police told us they had spent more time questioning Tracie. And they were keen to retrace the journey she and Lee had taken from the Marlbrook pub where they'd gone for a drink on the night of his murder.

DS Ian Johnston, who was leading the murder inquiry, asked if Ray, Michelle, Steve and I wanted to go with them. 'Tracie's coming,' he said. 'This isn't going to be easy for you but we need to get witnesses to come forward. If she gets through this, then we'd like to hold a press conference this afternoon.'

We didn't hesitate. No matter how hard we all knew it would be, we all needed to see for ourselves where Lee had died.

We met at the Hopwood pub on the outskirts of Birmingham. Tracie and her real dad John Andrews were in one of the police vans waiting when we arrived.

'Do you want to stop off on the way to buy some flowers?' I asked her.

The look on her face sent a shiver down my spine. It was a mixture of pure hatred and contempt. She was shaking violently. 'No!' she screamed at me. 'No, no, I don't.'

John stepped in between us and put his arms around her as she buried her face in his chest. She shrugged away my arm as I tried to comfort her.

'That'd be nice, Maureen,' John said. 'You get some for her.'

Following the police cars along the narrow winding lanes to Cooper's Hill, I knew that Ray, Michelle and Steve were all thinking the same thing. 'There's no way Lee would pull over down a pitch-black country lane,' said Ray. 'Not with a madman flashing his lights and giving him hand gestures when he didn't have to. An old lady in a Morris Minor could drive in the middle of this road and there is no way even Michael Schumacher could get round her. Tracie's story doesn't ring true.'

It was true, as we drove along the narrow country lanes, we kept having to brake at every corner just in case there was a car coming in the opposite direction. The steep mossy banks covered with tree roots on either side rose up like walls and the bare branches of the overhanging trees formed a dense canopy in places. At times, it felt almost as if we were driving through a tunnel.

As we slowly negotiated the final series of blind bends, I couldn't shake off Ray and Michelle's nagging doubts about Tracie's story. She'd told the police Lee had reached speeds of up to 70mph but we'd barely managed to get out of third gear. Nothing made sense any more.

When we pulled up behind the police cars in Cooper's Hill, I was struck by how peaceful the lane seemed. Keeper's Cottage, the house which overlooked the scene, couldn't be in a more idyllic setting. Flanked by woodland, it looked out from behind a tall box hedge over rolling pasture. It seemed impossible to believe that it was here, less than a mile from Tracie's flat, that Lee had taken his last breath.

Ray started to cry as he watched Michelle and I lay flowers on the grass verge next to the lane. There was no point trying to console him. For all of us, the grief was unbearable. The thought of knowing that we were standing just yards from where Lee's life had ended was just too much to take in.

As the four of us stood clinging to each other, I glanced over at the police van, expecting to see Tracie. She wouldn't get out. Even with the door open and John standing by it in the lane waiting for her, she was still sitting in the seat with her head bowed.

I watched as two police officers talked to her from outside and, after about five minutes, she climbed slowly out and stood staring at the ground as John put his arm round her. I could see she was shaking so much that she could hardly stand and, as John supported her, she continued to stare at the ground, never once raising her head.

After a couple of minutes, she put her hand back on the van door and half staggered, half collapsed back into the seat. As we watched the police van pull away, I couldn't help wondering if Tracie's reluctance to look at the place where she'd told police she'd held Lee in her arms for the last time as he lay dying was down to her grief or her guilt. Were her memories of what she'd witnessed too traumatic or was her reaction that of a cold-blooded killer who knew the police at the scene were closely watching her every move?

I have never felt so empty as I did on that cold December morning when I stood in Cooper's Hill. But, however shocking it was to picture Lee lying in the road, seeing where he'd died was an important part of trying to piece together the final moments of his life. I just hoped he hadn't suffered, and wanted to believe what the policeman on the phone had told me, that his death had been swift and painless after the fatal knife wound to his neck. Like the parent of any child who's been murdered, I wanted to know exactly what had happened to Lee.

After the intense pain of shock and sorrow, comes the overwhelming guilt that you weren't there to protect them. No matter how old they are, the primeval instinct to keep them from harm's way is always as powerful as the day they were born.

Lee was 25, but he was still my baby. My beautiful, precious little boy who had grown into a handsome young man. I wanted so much to believe that, even though he hadn't died in my arms, he had, at least, died in Tracie's. A woman, who in spite of all the heartache she'd caused him and our family during their relationship, had at least been there for him at the end.

Unlike Ray and Michelle, I didn't want to believe that she was the reason Lee was lying in a morgue. No matter how much I'd always disliked and mistrusted her or however unlikely her explanation about Lee's death seemed, my determination to believe her story was actually helping to keep me strong. Her bruised and swollen face was, at the time, all the proof I needed to convince me that she, too, had been a victim of the same senseless violence that had been unleashed on my son. Could the fact that Lee had died and she'd survived really make her a suspect?

Maybe the press conference would move things on and give the police a clearer picture of what had happened to Lee. And maybe we'd start getting nearer the truth, too.

4

Press Conference

Back at Redditch Police Station, prior to the press conference, Ray, Michelle, Steve and I were taken into a room where Tracie was sitting with Irene and Alan. Two policemen were talking to Tracie as she played with her hands and said nothing. We were offered tea as DS Ian Johnston came in.

'She's not going to do this, Alan,' Irene said, looking at us. 'Look at her, she can't do it.'

'Perhaps you can go in with her?' Ian Johnston said to Ray and me. 'For support.'

It was something we'd never considered being asked to do and the prospect of facing more reporters and photographers was really daunting. But we were just as keen as the police and press to hear her version of what happened for the first time. If her story didn't add up to us, we wanted to see what the reporters made of her.

I could see from the looks on Ray and Michelle's faces that they weren't happy. Just being in the same room as Tracie was too much for them.

'What would I have to do?' I asked Ian.

Tracie had told me not long after meeting Lee that she'd never been close to her mum. Any chance she'd had round at our house to run Irene down, she'd always made the most of it.

'She's not like you,' she'd told me on more than one occasion. 'We don't talk about things like you do with Lee and Michelle. Sometimes I wish you were my mum, Maureen. I don't think there's anything I couldn't say to you.'

Looking at Tracie, staring nervously round the room, wringing her hands and pulling the sleeves of her jumper down over her wrists, I couldn't imagine that she'd go through with it.

'I think Tracie just needs a bit of moral support,' said Ian. 'And I'll be in there with you.'

Tracie said nothing as I went over to her. 'Listen to me, I'll go in with you,' I told her. 'You're the star of this.'

It was almost as if a light had come on in Tracie's head as I described her as a star. She looked at me and nodded. There was no way she was going to miss out on her chance to perform for a captive audience.

'You're right, Maureen... I'm the star witness, aren't I?' she said. 'I've got to do this.'

Irene looked at Alan. 'You must do it, Tracie,' she said, sounding irritated.

Alan was gentler as he put his arm around her. 'Just put all your thoughts out of your head,' he said. 'You'll be fine.'

'I can't,' Tracie interrupted him and looked at Irene. I could see she was desperately seeking her mother's approval. 'Remember when I tried to...' Tracie started but stopped in mid-sentence as Irene glared at her.

'TRACIE!' she shouted, clearly irritated.

'Come on, I can stop it at any time,' Ian told Tracie. He was still looking at me as we all stood up. He was looking at his watch as he took hold of Tracie's arm. I sensed he was desperately trying to get her through the door so that she couldn't change her mind.

As I followed Ian to the door with Tracie, Ray stepped forward. 'I'll come in with you,' he said. 'We'll get through this together.'

The camera flashlights exploded as Ray and I followed Tracie into the packed room to where the media were waiting for their first glimpse of us. I could hardly catch my breath as Ray and I sat at a table next to her but, as I slowly looked around the room, I could see all eyes were on Tracie. They seemed fascinated by her.

Settling in the chair, I looked at the sea of faces in front of me and Tracie suddenly grabbed my hand. I felt her hand shaking and could see her staring at the floor as Ian introduced us. I couldn't believe this was actually happening. It felt like I was having an out-of-body experience.

Tracie said she and Lee had left the Marlbrook pub at around 9.45pm on the Sunday night in Lee's white 1990 Escort XR3i turbo car. On the way back to Tracie's flat in Alvechurch, a two-mile journey from the pub, she described how Lee had overtaken a tatty dark-coloured 1986 Ford Sierra, which then began a 'cat-and-mouse' chase. 'The car kept flashing its headlights and honking its horn at us,' she said. 'It was tail-gating us... we were driving at speeds of up to 70mph. I was shouting at Lee to slow down, to ignore them... But you know what a lot of men are like behind the wheel. Sometimes they change personality... They overtook us eventually and Lee stopped the car and got out.

'Lee and the Sierra driver, who was about 18 or 19, with short dark hair, were calling each other names and swearing at each other. They were pointing their fingers at each other and shouting. I kept yelling at Lee to get back into the car.

'I thought it was over when the driver started walking back to his car but, as he did, the passenger, who was white and very overweight, got out of the car and started attacking Lee. The guy was wearing a donkey jacket. He was older and fat and had staring eyes. He hit Lee several times. I got out of our car. I'm not the kind of person to sit there and just watch without doing anything. I was scared but I wanted him to stop.

'When I went to comfort Lee, the fat man called me a slut and punched me in the head. The driver was telling him to leave it. I didn't realise he'd used a knife on Lee. He was lying in the road and I knelt down beside him. He couldn't speak. I don't know if he was still alive. He wasn't breathing. I was trying to check for a pulse but I couldn't find one. I just tried to stop the bleeding and comfort him.'

Tracie kept looking down as the camera flashes kept going off.

'It's the most stupid, vile thing that's ever come out of a

car chase,' she continued. She was still hanging on to my hand as a reporter asked what Lee was like. 'Lovely,' she said. 'Kind, generous, funny... The man who did this has ruined my life and Ray and Maureen's.'

Ray choked back tears as the cameras flashed again. 'We're devastated,' he said. 'We're a close family. Lee was an honest, caring lad who tried to make the most of his life. We need capital punishment back. What I want to do is look into the eyes of my son's killer. If he's done it once, he can do it again. The next time, it could be your son, your daughter. I appeal to you to just turn him in... he deserves nothing better...' His voice broke as he tried to continue and he sat back with tears streaming down his face.

When another reporter, Rod Chaytor from the Daily Mirror, asked if Tracie could go over the timings of what had happened again, she stared at him, wild-eyed.

'What time did you say you and Lee left the Marlbrook pub, Tracie?' he asked her.

'It was about a quarter-to-ten,' she said.

'And yet the 999 call came in at 10.45?' he persisted. 'And it was a ten-minute journey to Cooper's Hill... is that right?

Tracie looked round and then helplessly at Ian Johnston. 'Yes, I think so. I think so, yes... I'm not exactly sure. Quarter-to-ten.'

For the first time during the press conference, Tracie looked rattled and stopped talking. Sensing her bewilderment, Ian Johnston came to her rescue. 'Obviously, we're still looking at this kind of detail,' he said. 'If there are no other questions, I think that's all for now.'

As we drove home, Ray and Michelle had a field day

going over what Tracie had said. 'It didn't take much to hang herself, did it?' Michelle insisted. 'It's obvious she's lying.'

'It was an Oscar-winning performance,' said Ray. 'Surely you saw that, Maureen? She never shed a tear until she was asked to go over the timing.'

Nothing I said to Ray and Michelle would make any difference. They'd made up their minds from the start and they couldn't understand why I was still determined to defend her. 'No one could be that good an actress,' I said. 'Not even Tracie.'

My heart was telling me that Ray and Michelle's suspicions about her being Lee's killer seemed far more likely, but in my head there was a little voice that kept telling me she was innocent. I didn't want to believe that she'd told a pack of lies and that she would put us through this nightmare to save her own skin. The police had said nothing to make me think otherwise. They knew what we were going through. Surely, if they thought Tracie had made up her story, they'd tell us. All I wanted was to give Tracie a chance to tell us the truth.

The next day, the tabloid newspapers went berserk with their coverage of the press conference. HACKED FROM EAR TO EAR said the headline in the *Daily Star*. ROADRAGE BLOODBATH said the *Sun*, while the *Daily Mirror* went for SLAUGHTERED.

Seeing ourselves on the television news bulletins made Lee's death real. It was the first time we'd ever been involved with the press and it was strange after reading so many similar stories about other families to see our photos and Lee's on the news.

Our phone never stopped ringing. Reporters wanting to

know if we'd give interviews, friends and family calling to ask if they could come over and see us. We didn't want to see anyone. We just wanted to be alone, to try to make sense of so much madness at a time when everyone else was getting ready for Christmas.

I don't know where we found the courage and strength to cope. Seeing the decorations, cards, Christmas trees and coloured lights festooned in all the shops... and, all the time, I seemed to be the only one who was prepared to give Tracie the benefit of the doubt. Even Anita wasn't taken in by Tracie's story. She told us that Danielle had been at Tracie's on the day Lee had been killed.

Tracie had arranged to take her and Carla to have some photographs taken at a local studio but, when Lee had offered to drop Danielle back at Anita's, Tracie had started arguing with him. The girls had told the police they'd heard a fierce row that afternoon and Tracie had told Lee she didn't trust him with Anita.

Just as Lee was convinced Tracie still fancied Carla's dad Andy, Tracie believed something was still going on between him and Anita. It was typical of the jealousy between them. Totally unfounded but enough to trigger another almighty row which ended after Tracie took both girls home without Lee – Carla to Irene's and Danielle to Anita's.

The fateful trip out to the Marlbrook pub that same evening had been an unsuccessful attempt to kiss and make up.

5

The Breakthrough

On Thursday, the day after the press conference, DS Mick O'Donnell and Brian Russell, our liaison officers, came to the house to take statements from Ray and me. The news they brought was far better than we could ever have hoped for so soon after the public appeal for witnesses.

Two people had come forward after seeing us on the television and reading the newspaper reports. It was a major breakthrough. The police had set up eight roadblocks on the Sunday night along the route that Tracie and Lee had taken. But, even though 120 of the 650 drivers questioned had been along the same roads over the weekend when Lee had been killed, none of them had seen the car chase that Tracie had described.

'What did they say?' I asked Brian. 'Did they see the other car? Surely you can tell us something?'

No matter how many questions we asked, Mick and Brian weren't able to answer any of them. It was vital nothing was leaked to the media at such a crucial stage in the inquiry, Mick told us. The less we knew about the witnesses, the less we could be tempted to say anything to the reporters who were camped outside our house. They'd also turned up at my hairdressing salon, asking staff about Lee and Tracie, and had even found out where Danielle went to school and had been chatting to pupils at the main gates, trying to find out who she was and what she looked like.

It was upsetting and annoying, but the story of Lee's death was so big that we knew nothing would stop journalists trying to find out as much as they could about him and Tracie. We had no intention of speaking to anyone but the police and our family. But we understood why the police had to keep the details of the witnesses under wraps. It was hard, but Ray and I knew we had to be patient; we had to put our trust in the police and wait.

The interviews for our statements were done separately and, as a formality, to eliminate us from the inquiry, we both had our fingerprints taken.

When they asked me if Lee carried a knife, I said the only one I'd ever known him own was when he'd been a member of the Boy's Brigade 13 years earlier. Alan Lee, the chap who ran the local Boy's Brigade group, had asked the parents of all the boys for their consent for him to give one to each of the boys, which the parents had paid for. As far as I knew, Lee had kept it in a box of memorabilia which I thought he'd taken to Tracie's.

They also asked about Lee and whether I'd thought he

was happy or was sometimes moody. I said Lee had been happy until he'd met Tracie and that, yes, he had been quite moody in the months before his death. I explained that he and Tracie had rowed constantly and had split up on several occasions, but, every time Lee left her and moved back home, Tracie would stalk him and constantly phone the house.

'They were very jealous of each other,' I said. 'They couldn't live together but they didn't seem to be able to live apart.'

'Did Lee have a temper?' Brian asked me.

'Tracie was always provoking him into arguments,' I said. 'She'd make a saint lose it. There were times when he gave as good as he got from her in shouting matches and throwing stuff, but he never hit her.

'Lee hated the way Tracie used to flirt with other men. It didn't matter what they looked like or how old they were, she was man-mad. Ask Lee's workmates, they'll tell you what she was like. If she had a chance to pick an argument and put Lee down in front of anyone, she would. He was sick of her behaviour but he'd just storm off. They were both jealous of each other.'

That day, Ray and I left no stone unturned in making sure the police knew everything that we did about Lee's relationship with Tracie.

Brian and Mick must have been amazed that we could recount so many rows and incidents in such detail, but it was a relief to be able to share what had been happening in our lives for the past two years. And, because Tracie's jealousy and temper had got the better of her on so many family occasions, it was easy to remember how upset we'd all been. I told Brian that Ray, Michelle and I had never liked Tracie. There was no point in being anything other than upfront about our feelings towards her.

All the conversations I'd ever had with her had confirmed our first impressions that growing up as the product of a broken home had left her massively insecure and deeply resentful. She'd told me, the first time we'd met, that men had always let her down. It was a pattern she blamed almost entirely on her dad John, who'd married Irene in 1963 and then split from her when Tracie was eight. She said she'd never been able to shake off the feeling of rejection after he left. And she was incredibly bitter about the fact that she didn't think he'd loved her enough to stay with Irene.

'I think that's why I turned into a bit of a bully at school,' she'd told me. 'If you hang round with people who are in control, they don't hurt you.'

She'd told me that, as a little girl, she'd only ever dreamed about becoming a model. The reality was actually far more mundane than Tracie liked, because she'd ended up working part-time in shops after leaving Bridley Moor High School in Redditch with six CSEs. The half-baked ambition she'd had to become a nurse disappeared in a pantomime puff of smoke when she'd joined a Youth Training Scheme working with the elderly.

'It was so sad, Maureen,' she'd said, checking her lipstick in our sitting-room mirror one evening while she was waiting for Lee to get ready to go out. 'I couldn't bear to see anyone in pain. It's a shame, really, because I'd have looked really good in a nurse's uniform.'

She met her first serious boyfriend Andy Tilston when she was 17 but, ten months after Carla was born, she walked out on him on her 22nd birthday after announcing that the wedding they'd been planning was off. Two years later, she moved into her council maisonette in Alvechurch and, after that, she sold hair and beauty products on a market stall in Birmingham.

'The other market traders used to call me the tart with the cart,' she giggled.

After she met Lee, she gave up working in the Kingfisher Centre in Redditch selling wigs and hairpieces – her one and only modelling job had been modelling hair extensions for a local hair salon – and started a job as a barmaid at the Red Lion pub near her flat. Lee had bought her an engagement ring in May 1995 but, two months later, Tracie threw him out of the flat after a row.

The warning signs about her violent nature had been there right from the start. Lee had only been seeing Tracie a couple of months when he came into the salon with his face covered in cuts and bruises.

'What the hell happened to you?' I asked him as he made himself a cup of tea in the back kitchen.

'Tracie,' he said. 'She had a mad one last night.' Lee explained they'd had a row and agreed to split up before going out for the evening. But Tracie had followed him to a nightclub where he'd gone with his mates. When she saw him talking with them at the bar, she'd launched herself at him with a broken beer bottle, spitting at him and swearing as his mates struggled to pull her off.

On another occasion, after yet another row, about a

month before Lee's death, Tracie had seen him talking to a barmaid and bit him on the neck. Later the same night, she went up to him again and punched him twice on the side of the head. 'You can buy me a fucking drink for this,' she'd told Lee.

Ray and I couldn't believe our eyes when Lee turned up and showed us the circle of ugly teeth marks and gashes on his neck. He looked as though he'd been savaged by a wild animal. When Lee met Andy Tilston, one of the first things he warned Lee about Tracie was her violent temper.

I told Brian that Lee had told me how Andy had mentioned being attacked by Tracie on several occasions and had once even pulled a knife on him. His words had struck such a chord at the time. He said she would be like a wolf when she freaked out. She always seemed to go for the neck.

The extreme behaviour Tracie often displayed when she and Lee were alone together was, in many ways, as spiteful and destructive as the mood swings we'd put up with when Lee brought her home. Tracie would seize on an innocent remark and blow it up into a full-scale argument. When Michelle and Steve announced their engagement at a family barbecue, Tracie stormed off into the house in tears.

No one knew she and Lee had been talking about getting married, but Tracie was convinced Michelle and I had hatched a plot between us to make sure that Michelle and Steve pipped them to the post. It was a ridiculous childish reaction but, even when I tried to tell Tracie that she'd got the wrong idea, there was no consoling her.

'Michelle's got to get in there before Lee and me, hasn't

she?' she yelled. 'She's spoiled our surprise. We were going to tell the family about our engagement but now they can stuff it.'

Michelle knew Tracie's reaction was simply because she wasn't the centre of attention, but I was angry. It should have been a wonderful and memorable day for her but Tracie had set out to try to ruin things with her jealousy.

It had been exactly the same with Michelle's wedding, even though we'd gone out of our way to make sure that Tracie felt she was welcome to be part of it. She and Lee kept falling out and getting back together again so we didn't know if they'd be together for the wedding. Having asked Carla to be a bridesmaid with Paige and Danielle, because of Lee, Michelle told him that she and Steve needed to know what was happening with Tracie so they could get Carla's dress made.

Lee understood this and told her not to bother having Carla as a bridesmaid, but, when he and Tracie got back together, Tracie asked if Carla could be a bridesmaid again. Michelle said yes again, but said it was their last chance to finalise it because they obviously couldn't keep being messed about.

It didn't take them long to have yet another row and split up and, this time, Michelle and Steve decided they'd had enough and told Lee that Carla couldn't be a bridesmaid but they would all be welcome at the wedding.

When Tracie realised they'd said no to Carla, she said she wouldn't be coming. Michelle and Steve couldn't have cared less. But, when Tracie and Lee had another row and then got back together, Tracie made it a condition that she'd only go back with Lee if he didn't attend the wedding.

Lee explained this to Michelle and hoped she'd understand that he was planning a future with Tracie. Michelle wasn't very happy because, naturally, she and Steve had wanted Lee to be there, but there wasn't much any of us could do about it.

Ray phoned Tracie as the wedding date got nearer and asked her to think about what she was asking Lee to do and to change her mind and let him come.

'It's got nothing to do with me,' she'd told him. 'Lee can do what he wants.'

I knew exactly what was going on in Tracie's twisted mind. She just couldn't stand the thought of Michelle and Steve's big day overshadowing her own. It was a shame for Carla because she hadn't been a bridesmaid before and had been really excited about the prospect of going down the aisle with Danielle, Paige and Michelle.

I was too angry to cry when Lee told us Tracie had given him an ultimatum. It was evil, the kind of incomprehensible and irrational thought process that set Tracie apart from the rest of the world. Tracie knew how much Lee and Michelle loved each other and how much it meant to all of us to be together on such a special day, but she'd set out to destroy it.

I look back and wonder how I ever managed to tolerate Tracie's deluded sense of self-importance. Why hadn't I just gone round to her flat and given her a good hard slap across the face? I think I just never expected Lee to give in to her. If he really couldn't be there on his sister's wedding day because of Tracie, then nothing would come between them.

From that moment on, I refused to speak to Tracie or have anything to do with her. Lee did come to the house on the morning of the wedding to bring presents for Michelle and Steve. He said he was sorry he wasn't going to be there but gave his sister a massive hug and told her he loved her. It should have been a day when, as we all hugged each other, the tears we shed should have been tears of joy, not sorrow.

I'm sure even his mates couldn't understand how Tracie managed to wield so much emotional power over Lee. We certainly couldn't.

As I told Brian and Mick that day, she was convinced that Lee was her Mr Right. Even though the pattern of their relationship was established early on – rowing, splitting up, reconciling – they couldn't go without each other for more than a few days. When Lee had called off the engagement, six months after they'd had a party to announce they were getting married, I told them Tracie had called at our house every day. Within a fortnight, he was back living with her again. No matter how much her sulking and explosive rages drove Lee to distraction, he was completely infatuated with her.

'If you don't stop seeing each other, you'll end up killing each other,' Michelle had told Lee, after he turned up at home one morning with an ugly scratch running the length of one side of his face. That had happened just six months before Lee's death.

Lee had laughed. 'It's only a scratch,' he'd said. 'She just loses it. It's the way she is.'

It was something that Tracie had openly joked about in front of us. Watching the video Fatal Attraction at our house one evening, she feigned a stabbing motion into a cushion on the settee next to Lee after the scene where the mistress is trying to kill her married lover. 'I'd be just like that,' she declared, whacking Lee in the face with the cushion. 'If I couldn't have you, then I certainly wouldn't let anyone else.'

About a week later, we were watching television when details of a chilling road-rage incident in Kent came on the news. Stephen Cameron and his fiancée had been driving off a slip road on to the M25 when another driver had stopped them and attacked Stephen. He'd died from a knife wound to the heart.

'God, Lee, that could have been us,' Tracie said. 'They're good-looking like us… he's dark and she's blonde.'

Finding a child-minder to look after Carla had obviously given Tracie far more freedom than when she'd relied on Irene. I couldn't understand why the poor kid spent so much time with the woman. Tracie only worked part-time and, even when she wasn't going out, she seemed to prefer not having Carla around. Maybe she thought being a mum was all about dressing her like a doll in frilly ankle socks and hair ribbons rather than spending time with her.

'She likes being at her house more than she does here,' Tracie said, when I asked her why Carla was spending Christmas Day with her childminder. 'She's a really nice woman and is really good with kids. They do all sorts of stuff together. You should be pleased I'm getting to spend so much time with Lee.'

But there were plenty of times when Tracie would go out without even telling him what her plans were. She'd tell him to pick her up and would often be out when he did. When he had chicken pox and was living with Tracie, she'd even told him he'd just have to fend for himself. Just because he was off work and in bed, itching and covered from head to toe in sores, didn't mean she had to stay in. After just a couple of days, she told him that, if he wasn't up to going out on Friday, he might as well come home to Ray and me.

'I'm not your fucking nursemaid,' she told him.

Typically, she'd packed Carla off to her childminder, put on her slap and high heels and told Lee she didn't know when she'd be back.

It was an entirely different matter if Tracie was ever ill. She only had to get a mild headache and the world would have to stand still while she went to bed.

When Danielle came to stay with us for the weekend, I usually offered to have Carla because they enjoyed each other's company so much. There were a couple of occasions when Danielle stayed at Tracie's when it was Lee's weekend to have her. But, when the rows between her and Lee seemed to get more and more regular, I stopped letting her go. I knew Lee would never let her witness any violent confrontations or listen to Tracie's foul-mouthed temper tantrums, but I couldn't risk it.

When Brian asked Ray and me why we thought Tracie had always had such a hold over Lee, the only reason we could come up with was the sex, and the fact that he couldn't bear the thought of her leaving him or being physically intimate with another man. She loved to make Lee jealous, especially in front of his friends. I couldn't remember a single occasion when Lee hadn't come home and described her provocative dancing with blokes who thought she was out clubbing alone. If Lee ignored her behaviour, she'd go up to someone on the dance floor who was dancing with another girl and start dancing in between them.

In my day, she'd have been described as a prick-tease. It was the only way she knew of getting attention – the short skirts, skimpy tops and high heels got her noticed. It didn't matter that she wasn't particularly bright and only talked about things she watched on the telly or make-up and hair products she'd seen in magazines and wanted to try. She was a tarty blonde with a half-decent face and figure. What else did she need to get attention in a busy pub or nightclub?

Any hopes we'd had that Lee would come to his senses and end their relationship were dashed in June 1996 when Tracie discovered she was pregnant.

It was last thing we'd expected but Lee was over the moon and Tracie lapped up the attention when they came round for a meal to tell us.

'It's great, isn't it?' she said. 'A little brother or sister for Danielle and Carla. We can't wait, can we, Lee?'

They both seemed so delighted that Ray and I wondered whether having a baby might force them to take a more mature attitude to their relationship. It might even be the making of them once they realised just how much hard work and responsibility would be needed to look after a little one.

But, at the back of my mind, there were nagging doubts about how Tracie would cope with pregnancy when her life revolved around going out to have a good time. Lee had already proved himself as a hands-on dad to Danielle but he knew he'd only been able to do his bit because Anita was such a brilliant mum and Ray, Michelle, Steve and I were always around to help out. And would Tracie feel the same way when her bump got so big she could no longer fit into her skimpy outfits.

It was a worrying prospect, especially as the pregnancy was unplanned and Tracie rarely went out of her way to spend more time than she had to with Carla.

Two months later, it seemed that fate had stepped in to end all the uncertainty. Irene rang and said Tracie fallen down some steps while she'd been out shopping in Redditch. She was four months pregnant and had suffered a miscarriage. Irene said Tracie was so devastated that she'd told her mum to make sure we didn't turn up at the Alexandra Hospital where she said she'd been taken by ambulance. She couldn't even face seeing Lee.

We all went over to her flat to see her the next day. I'd never seen Tracie looking as vulnerable and upset as she was that day. Hollow-eyed and sobbing as she sat next to Lee on the settee, she was convinced it was all her fault. No matter how much we tried to console her and tell her they could always try again, she told us she was convinced the miscarriage was a punishment. It took the best part of a month for Tracie to put losing the baby behind her and resume hostilities with Lee.

Lee was certain her dramatic weight loss – nearly two stones in six weeks – was a result of her miscarriage, but I wasn't convinced. She was definitely eating less but didn't appear to have lost her enthusiasm for clubbing and drinking. If anything, she was far more obsessed about her appearance than she had ever been and had even sent away for brochures on cosmetic surgery. It didn't take me long to work out what she'd got in mind. What better excuse to get Lee to stump up the money for a boob job than the trauma of losing the baby?

'Even Lee thinks my boobs aren't what they were,' she told me. 'All this weight I've lost has made them go really flat.'

She'd been seeing Lee less than a year when she started going on about wanting a breast enlargement. From the moment she knew he had some shares with West Midlands Travel where he worked as a bus driver, she was like a dog with a bone. *He* would be the one to benefit if he cashed them in and gave her the money for a boob job, she'd told him. With bigger breasts, she'd said, he'd fancy her even more and, who knows, they might even get her the modelling break she was convinced was just around the corner.

I told Lee I thought he was mad even to think about throwing away his hard-earned cash on her and he never mentioned it again.

One afternoon, not long after the miscarriage, she turned up with Lee for lunch and started going on about her boobs. They were obviously swollen with milk, hardly the kind of topic I'd have expected her to mention at the dinner table, but it didn't stop her embarrassing Ray.

'What do you think, Ray?' she laughed. 'I suit them bigger, don't I?'

Ray didn't know where to look, let alone what to say. I could see Tracie was enjoying his embarrassment. Lee said nothing.

'Come on,' she went on, grabbing Ray's hands and planting them on her breasts. 'Have a good feel and tell me what you think. They're enormous, aren't they?'

Talking to the police about Tracie that day and going over everything that we'd had to put up with really helped all of us to put things into perspective. She'd caused so much unhappiness with her selfish behaviour and yet I'd gone on accepting her for Lee's sake. Tracie knew how much we all loved him, but seemed to take a perverse pleasure from watching us tread on eggshells when she was around. We'd had no option but to put up with her. We couldn't risk losing Lee. And, no matter how bad the arguments between them were, he was always prepared to give Tracie one more chance.

In the September before he'd died, he'd spent a small fortune taking her, Danielle and Carla on holiday to Portugal and, when she told him he should be spending more time with her, he'd even given up his bus-driving job.

He'd loved his job as a bus driver for West Midlands Travel and was just as popular with the regulars who travelled on his route as he was with the other drivers. One of the funniest things I remember was when Lee had been for a curry with the lads the night before an early shift. He'd been at work for a while when, all of a sudden, I heard a key in the front door and someone running upstairs – it was Lee. When he came down, I asked him if he wanted a cuppa but he said that he couldn't stop because he was working. He'd been so desperate to go to the toilet that he'd parked the bus, locked the twirlies on it and run through the gully home! He used to call the pensioners 'twirlies' because they would always try to use their passes on the bus before 9.30, asking, 'Am I too early, driver?' All the old girls who were on his route loved him and used to say, 'If only I was a few years younger...'

Typically, he and Tracie seeing more of each other only served to fan the flames and, not long afterwards, I'd had a call from Irene one night asking me to come and get Lee. When I turned up at the flat, Tracie was hysterical saying that Lee had punched her and thrown hi-fi equipment at her. I knew she was lying. Lee might have lost it and started chucking stuff around but he'd never hit her.

'Just get him out of here,' Irene shouted at me, as Lee started picking up some of his things. 'I can't cope with any more of this.'

'It's OK, we're going,' I yelled at Tracie. 'And, this time, make sure you bloody well stay away from Lee. Don't even think about stalking him and phoning the house like you usually do. It's finished. Just stay away from him.'

Outside the flat, I told Lee to get in the car but he just ignored me and walked off. A few yards down the road, I found him sitting on a wall with his head in his hands and stopped the car. 'You don't want to know me, do you?' he asked.

He looked terrible. I wanted to take him in my arms and tell him everything was going to be all right. 'How many more times are you going to let Tracie treat you like this?' I asked him.

Lee shrugged his shoulders and got into the passenger seat next to me. 'It's over this time, Mum,' he said. 'Take me home.'

'And he still went back after all that?' Brian asked.

I nodded. The rest was history, I told him. Ray and I had begged him to stay at home and have nothing more to do with Tracie. 'If only he'd listened to us, none of this would have happened,' I told him. 'Lee wouldn't be lying in a morgue... he'd have been sitting here with us today.'

Later that same day, Michelle and I went back to Cooper's Hill. It was something we knew neither of us could do alone but together it just seemed right. And, although neither of us mentioned it until we got into the car, we wanted to have a look round and see if we could find the knife.

It sounds mad when I think about it now. The idea that the two of us could find the murder weapon after a load of forensics officers had been scouring the area looking for it since the night of Lee's death. I guess you do some strange things when you're trying to cope with shock and grief. We just wanted to feel that we were doing something to help.

The police had cut back all the hedgerows and bushes at the side of the lane where Lee had stopped his car. The white tent that had covered the area where he'd been found had gone. Michelle and I poked around in the roadside ditches and in the hedges for the best part of an hour looking for the knife. There was no one else about but we were on such a mission that I don't think we'd have noticed anyway.

We both had a cry as we stood overlooking the fields from the lane. The two of us standing side by side, lost in thought as we remembered how much Lee had loved the weeks leading up the Christmas. The present buying, the parties, going out with his mates, putting up the decorations with Danielle at our house. It was definitely a favourite time of year in the Harvey household.

'I think Christmas is cancelled this year, eh, Mum?' Michelle sighed as we walked back to her car.

It was another heartbreaking reminder of how all our lives had been changed. We'd lost Lee and yet we still had two little girls, Paige and Danielle, who now, more than any other time, needed to know that Christmas was still a magical time.

6

Suicide Bid

When we got home, the news that came in a phone call from Ian Johnston was the last thing we'd expected.

'Tracie's taken an overdose,' Ian told me on the phone. 'She was at her mum's flat. She'd written suicide notes for Irene and Carla and said she couldn't carry on without Lee. She took about 200 pills, so she'd have succeeded if Brian hadn't called round to the house and found her this afternoon. She's going to be all right. She's gone to the Alex Hospital. They've pumped her stomach but we're keeping an eye on her in case she tries it again.'

Ray, Michelle and Steve were elated, almost dancing round the sitting room as they hugged each other, but I was so shocked I burst into tears. I didn't know what to say. I didn't want to carry on without Lee but I had more guts than to shove a load of pills down my neck and leave my family without a wife, a mum and a grandmother. It seemed such a selfish and callous thing to do, a coward's way of escaping and leaving the rest of us to try to make sense of losing Lee.

'She bloody well knows the police are on to her,' said Ray. 'Surely you can see this proves she's guilty, Maureen. The little bitch can't live with herself.'

I was stunned. Had Brian suspected she was planning this? I wondered. 'He must have gone over to Irene's after he and Mick left us,' I said.

How scared must Tracie have been to try to take her own life? She had no way of knowing about the two witnesses who had contacted the police. Why would she try to top herself if she had nothing to hide? For the first time since being told about Lee, I couldn't defend Tracie. But I still didn't want to believe that a failed overdose was an admission of guilt.

It was horrendous to think of the consequences for her daughter Carla if she'd succeeded. I couldn't get my head around the idea that she would have decided to leave an innocent child without her mum rather than face the consequences of her actions.

Ray and I drove straight to the hospital where Brian explained he'd found her collapsed on the bed at her mum's. 'She told her mum she was going for a sleep and I went in to wake her. If I hadn't got there when I did, she wouldn't be here,' he said. 'She meant business when she took those pills.'

Ray and I walked into the room where Tracie was lying with her eyes closed in a hospital bed. There were two uniformed police officers standing outside the room. Were they there to make sure she didn't try it again or because Tracie was now the main murder suspect?

Irene and Alan Carter were sitting by the side of the bed as we went in and pulled up chairs. They looked terrible. Irene couldn't look at me for more than a few seconds. Alan acknowledged us with a nod and squeezed Tracie's hand.

'Why don't you two go and get a coffee?' I suggested. 'Ray and I will stay with her until you get back. You both look as though you could do with a break.'

Irene's face was filled with panic as I stepped forward to hug Tracie. 'NO!' she shouted. 'We're staying. It's OK.'

'I'll be OK, Mum...' Tracie's voice was barely a whisper. 'Go and get a coffee like Maureen says. I'm not going anywhere.'

Irene raked her hand through her hair, looked at Alan and then reluctantly followed him out of the room.

'How are you feeling, bab?' I asked Tracie.

She turned her head away and closed her eyes.

'What about if we went away for a couple of days?' I asked. 'It might help. We could take Danielle and Carla with us. Just you and me.'

Suddenly, Tracie turned and clutched both my hands, tears spilled over into the dark circles beneath her eyes as she looked into my eyes. 'Sorry, Maureen,' she whispered. 'I'm sorry for what I have done.' She sobbed as I held her in my arms just as Irene and Alan came back into the room.

My head was spinning. What had Tracie meant? I was desperate to ask her if she was referring to her suicide attempt or to what had happened to Lee.

'Come on, she needs to get some rest,' said Alan. Irene was staring at Tracie. 'We can get a coffee later.'

'We've brought something which might help you,' I said. I slid the package out of my bag and undid it. 'I've had these photos enlarged for you. There's one of Lee and that one of the two of you together when we went for a meal at The Gate Hangs Well.'

Tracie took one look at the head-and-shoulders photograph of Lee and began to shake. Her eyes were darting wildly across the image as she buried her face in her hands and sobbed. 'Get these photos out of here, Mum,' she screamed. 'And go to my flat and get rid of all Lee's things. I want them out of my flat before I go home.' Tracie sank back into the pillows and turned her face away from us. I could sense the tension between her and Irene.

'We'll come back and see you tomorrow,' I told her. 'Try and get some sleep.'

Irene said she'd take the photographs I'd had done of Lee and Tracie and keep them safe until she was strong enough to see them.

Outside the room, Ray put his arm around me as one of the police closed the door. 'She's as guilty as hell, Maureen,' he said, shaking his head. 'I think that's the nearest thing you and I are going to get to hearing a confession.'

We told Brian what Tracie had said to us and how she'd reacted when I'd shown her the photographs. As we stood chatting with some of the police in the hospital corridor, Irene came out of the room with Alan. She hardly glanced at Ray and me as she walked further along the corridor.

We followed them, watching Irene fumbling in her

handbag for her cigarettes. 'I'm going to need a good drink when we get home,' she told Alan. She shook as she lit a cigarette and inhaled deeply.

At home that night, Ray, Michelle, Steve and I sat up most of the night going over what had happened. We were all exhausted but none of us could think about trying to sleep. Michelle and Steve hadn't gone home. Somehow, it helped just being together, but the more I listened to Ray and Michelle, the angrier I felt. If Ray was right and Tracie had been on the verge of confessing to killing Lee at the hospital, what the hell were the police playing at? Why hadn't they arrested her if she was the main suspect? How could she have tried to fool us all at the press conference? The only thing left in my mind as I remembered how she'd clung to my hand was that she was trying to save her own neck. I still didn't want to believe what to Ray and Michelle was staring us all in the face – that Tracie Andrews was a killer.

The call from Ian Johnston, when it came on Saturday morning, 7 December, was enough to make us realise that he had some vital information for us.

'I can't talk to you on the phone,' he said. 'I need to come and see you straight away.'

Why would the most senior policeman in the inquiry want to make a special trip to see us? Tracie had spent two days at the Alexandra Hospital in Redditch recovering from her suicide bid.

When Ian Johnston arrived 20 minutes later, we had no idea what he was going to tell us. I was shaking as I let him in and sat next to Ray on the settee.

'I don't know whether or not you're aware of this but

Tracie's being discharged from hospital this morning,' he began. 'And, as I speak, she is being arrested in connection with Lee's murder. I can't tell you too much but the witnesses who responded to our appeal are a couple who saw Lee's car travelling along the lane to Cooper's Hill. Tracie is our main suspect now.'

Ray and Michelle hugged each other as I sat sobbing on the settee. I couldn't take any of it in. Suddenly, we were all firing questions at him. Ray and Michelle shook Ian's hand. It was the first time that week I'd seen either of them laugh. Their suspicions had finally been confirmed. They had been right about Tracie all along.

'Are you sure about this?' I asked him. 'Is there new evidence?'

Ian nodded. 'I'm afraid I can't tell you much more. The facts will all come out when she appears in court.'

I wanted to feel relieved, to share Ray and Michelle's elation, but all I really wanted was my son back. I didn't want to be sitting there in tears, feeling so confused, angry and upset, hardly able to take in the reality of what Ian Johnston was telling us. I couldn't believe that Tracie had lied. She'd sat there as I held her hand like a bloody fool and felt sorry for her. And now I had to get my head around the fact that this evil scheming woman, who I'd never wanted in our lives, had not only murdered Lee, she'd also betrayed me. She'd thrown my trust straight back in my face.

Whatever else we had to face, nothing mattered now. I just wanted to get justice for Lee, to make her pay for what she'd done to my son. To see her rot in hell.

The press were told by the police that a 27-year-old

woman had been arrested in connection with the murder inquiry into Lee's death. Obviously, Tracie couldn't be named at that stage but it didn't stop the media putting two and two together and, within an hour of the arrest being made, reporters, photographers and film crews started rolling back into our road.

I went over to tell Anita what was happening and had planned to bring Danielle back to our house for tea. But, thankfully, before I turned into the driveway, Babs and her daughter Donna stopped me in their car and explained that we needed to make a detour so the photographers wouldn't see Danielle. There was no way I was going to take Danielle back to Anita's so soon after promising her tea with her nan, so, instead, we drove to a local Wacky Warehouse and stayed there for a couple of hours.

Father Christmas was there and, when she asked Babs and me if she could tell him what she wanted him to bring her, we both wondered what the big man with the white beard might promise.

I knew she'd asked Lee for Tiny and Tim twin dolls but, when she scrambled on to Father Christmas's knee and he asked her what she'd like, I thought my heart was going to break.

'I'd like you to bring my daddy home,' she told him.

She was too young to understand the enormity of Lee's death and, even in the car on the way home, she wanted to know if he'd be there waiting for us.

'Everything your mum's told you about Daddy being in heaven is true,' I told her. 'He loves you very much and always will and he'll be watching over you.'

'I know, Nan,' she said. 'I've seen his star from my bedroom window.'

7

Closing in on a Killer

For 11 days, Tracie remained under police guard in a psychiatric facility, the Reaside Hospital in Rubery on the outskirts of Birmingham. While she was undergoing psychiatric assessments, the police called for a news blackout on the case. Speculation about who Lee's killer was became rife.

Suddenly, Tracie's story seemed riddled with flaws. There were still no witnesses to the car chase she'd described and, thanks to regular visits from Brian and Mick, we knew the police were also puzzled about where blood was found around Lee's car. They were also very interested in the statements made by Susan Duncan, an ex-CID police officer who lived in Keeper's Cottage on Cooper's Hill, and her friend who'd been with her that evening and who had found Tracie with Lee as he left to go home.

A couple of days after Tracie's arrest, Andy Tilston turned up at our home and said he was planning to give a statement to the police about his relationship with Tracie. We couldn't believe that he seemed prepared to go into the witness box and speak out against the mother of his little girl. But he was so shocked by her arrest and Lee's death that he said he'd made up his mind to tell them about the time she'd tried to attack him with a bread knife after a row.

'What's happened to your Lee could have happened to me,' he said sadly. 'She really lost it with me. If I hadn't managed to get the knife off her, I'm not sure I'd have been here. Nothing I did for Tracie was ever good enough. She smothered me with her insecurity and just wouldn't leave it if she thought she was being ignored. It's only right that the police find out what she's capable of before this goes to court.'

It was music to our ears. It took the best part of 24 hours after that for him to change his mind about making a statement. The day afterwards, he came round to see us with a friend and brought Carla. She didn't need to hear us discussing her mum so I told her to go and play in Danielle's bedroom while we chatted to her dad downstairs.

'I'm so sorry, I can't go through with this statement,' he said. 'If I appear as a witness, I may not be able to see Carla again. I can't risk that happening.'

There was no point trying to force Andy to change his mind. We'd tell the police about it and leave it to them to decide what action to take.

It was strange saying goodbye to Carla. It was the last

time we ever got to speak to her. None of this was her fault; she hadn't asked for a mother with a heart of stone.

I spent that week escaping from everything at home. Ray was using brandy as his emotional anaesthetic and crying himself to sleep. And I'd had enough of the endless cups of tea and sandwiches and the nosier members of our extended family who all seemed to want to offer their own verdict on Tracie's guilt. I had to get away from the constantly ringing phone and the police coming and going to make sure we were coping.

Even though my hairdressing salon had become a mission control for the gossips, it was the only sanctuary I had. Michelle and I had opened the Hair Company in King's Heath in 1995. It was doing well because we had some loyal clients who liked to pamper themselves. Many were women I'd known for years.

Ever the opportunist, Tracie had tried to get in on the act by asking Lee to sell his shares in West Midlands Travel where he'd worked so she could buy a share of the salon and work with us. We'd spent loads of money converting it from a shop which had sold sweets and cut-price cigarettes. Steve had rewired it and put in all the plumbing and fittings and Ray's cousin made a fantastic job of the black-and-white tiling.

I can remember Tracie breezing in when all the hard work had been done, the day before we were due to open, and bragging about how she'd worked as a hair stylist a few years before meeting Lee. At the time, she was selling wigs and hairpieces in the Merry Hill shopping centre and working part-time as a barmaid, but she said hairdressing had always been her dream job.

We knew she'd had no formal training and had no intention of asking her to join us but, a few weeks after we'd opened, Lee rang and asked me if we'd give Tracie a try. I told him straight that it wouldn't work. Michelle and I couldn't stand her and she was the last person either of us would want as a business partner. It caused a huge row between Lee and Tracie but, after that, she never showed her face at the salon again.

Before opening the Hair Company, I'd run six salons of my own in the Birmingham area. I loved my job and had always wanted to open my own salon since I'd trained as a stylist after leaving school in 1961. It was hard work and the hours were long but the financial rewards were worth it. And there was always something to have a laugh about with the clients.

Michelle had told me she wanted to train as a stylist after leaving school but I tried to talk her out of it because I wanted her to do something a bit more challenging. But she was adamant and had turned out to be a real natural at the job. The customers loved her because she was always so laidback, full of fun and happy to listen to the stories they always shared with us while they were having their hair done.

I don't know what it is about hairdressers but they do seem to bring out the home truths and confidences of total strangers. Especially when it comes to comparing notes on each other's sex lives. Idle chitchat often turned to graphic descriptions of bedroom conquests and dating disasters, menopausal moments of madness with toy-boys and unrequited passion in the typing pool.

Like all hairdressers who generally find themselves on the receiving end of so many client confidences, I cut, permed, rolled and back-combed without batting an eyelid at their revelations. One customer happily confessed to enjoying a passionate affair with her best friend's husband and then, a few weeks later, the best friend poured her heart out to me about her husband's infidelity. Both women were regular clients and yet neither of them had any idea I'd been given both sides of the story and knew exactly which bed the philandering husband was spending more time in.

I knew it would be hard to face everyone when I went back to the salon a few days after Lee's death, especially as the staff were getting hassled by the press. Kim had done a great job keeping the place ticking over, but I knew I'd have to help her juggle the appointments while Michelle and I were out of the frame. Even if our lives were on hold, the rest of the world were getting on with theirs. And we couldn't afford simply to let things fall apart when it was our busiest time of the year. The brown envelopes were still coming through the letterbox. We still had bills to pay.

What I hadn't realised was that so many people would want to know everything about the investigation. Everyone who came in had an opinion about Tracie and, even when I tried to explain that we couldn't talk about the case because the police weren't telling us anything, the questions kept coming thick and fast. They wanted a haircut for a fiver and my personal tragedy for free.

One afternoon, two women stood staring into the salon as I was doing someone's hair. When the door opened, one of them said, 'There she is. She's the one whose son's been murdered.'

Even the sandwich man who used to come into the salon had an opinion.

'His girlfriend knows someone who works at the Alex Hospital,' said Kim one morning. 'She saw Tracie and Lee when they were brought in and said Lee had been stabbed 32 times.'

I couldn't believe what I was hearing. 'Lee was stabbed 42 times,' I said angrily. 'When he comes in next time, tell him to get his bloody facts right. In fact, tell him not to bother coming again.'

There were times when I could hardly bear to talk to the customers and often walked into the back room to have a good cry when they started asking me how I was coping. The thought of picking up a razor to style someone's hair left me cold. All I could think about was the image of Lee being stabbed.

It didn't take me long to work out who the genuine ones were but those who booked appointments just to quiz me about what was happening with Tracie didn't get away lightly. If the nosey buggers wanted to tell their friends they'd had their hair done 'by the woman whose son had been murdered', then I'd make them pay for it.

'Oooh, yes,' I'd say as they smiled back at me in the mirror. 'But I won't have time to tell you everything if you're just having a trim... why don't I do you a perm or a cut-and-blow-dry?'

Back at home, Ray's sisters and mine would take it in turns to arrive with food parcels and settle in for the day. I knew they meant well but, at the time, it felt like we were being taken over. Alan and Babs were the only ones who really understood what we were going through. They came every day and stayed and I hope they both know how much having them with us helped.

Alan really got on with Mick O'Donnell. Like us, he'd recognised a sensitive and caring man who was able to put us all at ease and knew how important it was to keep updating us with information about the inquiry.

Barbara, my sister, who's even more house-proud than me – and anyone who knows me will probably find this hard to believe – couldn't stop bloody hoovering. She was in her element. My house is always immaculate and the last thing we all needed was her going over all the carpets in the house when they were already spotless.

Josie, my other sister, was on a mission to turn the kitchen into a greasy-spoon café. 'I know you won't have had a chance to get any food in,' she'd say, bustling into the hallway with carrier bags heaving with groceries. 'You've got to eat to keep your strength up. I've got some nice crusty bread, some bacon, some sausages and eggs. Who fancies a nice sandwich?'

I can remember watching her frying away in the kitchen, bacon fat splashing all over my nice clean cooker, and thinking, I don't want a bloody sandwich.

I think we must have broken the world tea-drinking record several times over and God knows how many times I rolled up my sleeves and washed up. But we didn't need it. It was all for our families' benefit, not ours. A way of trying to mask the awkwardness of not knowing what to say to us.

I knew I wasn't the only one who felt the same way. Michelle was doing her best not to show how irritated she was but I knew she just wanted everyone to go. If there wasn't someone sitting on the settee drinking endless cups of tea, there was someone answering the phone, folding tea towels, washing the kitchen floor.

'I just need to have five minutes alone with Mum and Dad,' Michelle would say diplomatically. She kept a lot to herself during those dark days after Tracie's arrest. We all did. But there were times when, after everyone had gone, she would just break her heart and dissolve into floods of tears. I felt so helpless and lost.

What got us through was just the four of us being together. Michelle and Steve didn't want to go home and Ray and I were glad when they said they'd stay in the spare room. Every evening, Ray would drink his way through a bottle of brandy. One minute, he'd be laughing, the next he'd be sobbing like a baby. I was worried because, even though I knew it was his way of trying to escape, the drinking was making him moody and, at times, irrational and extremely angry. We were all feeling so much pain, so much anger, that we didn't know how to deal with the grief.

My GP offered me tranquillisers but I refused to take them. There didn't seem to be any point in trying to blot out the trauma with drugs when a glass of brandy or the odd gallon or two of tea did much the same job.

In some ways, it was easier to relate to our liaison officers than our own family. We grew to love them all for different reasons and really appreciated their friendship and professionalism. Brian would always make us laugh, regaling us with stories about his wife and two daughters and telling us about his mum and how proud she was of him. She'd even send us chocolate biscuits when she knew he was coming to see us and he told us he was under strict instructions from her to look after us. He was a good sport and a bit of a ladies' man, so we were always pulling his leg about his good looks.

Steve Walters was the most senior officer and, while he always seemed a bit more guarded when we talked about the case, his courtesy and kindness was a measure of his sensitivity and integrity. Like his boss, Ian Johnston, he commanded respect and trust among his colleagues and was the one who always went out of his way to reassure us that his team would bring Lee's killer to justice.

Ian won Michelle over from the start. She hung on his every word and would often challenge his views about how the case was progressing. His natural air of authority was a great source of reassurance to all of us and his experience made it easy to trust him.

8

Charged

At 10.00pm on 19 December, Tracie was charged with Lee's murder after being questioned at Redditch Police Station. Her solicitor Tim Robinson made a statement outside the station which was televised on the evening news: 'My client continues to vehemently deny any involvement with the murder of her boyfriend,' he said. 'I don't believe the police are looking for anyone else in connection with the death and that is the case they are putting to Miss Andrews. It's a theory that is flawed, full of holes and not substantiated.'

Like us, the police were confident Tracie would remain in custody after she appeared at Redditch Magistrates Court the day after being charged. But, during the three-hour hearing, Tim Robinson asked for reporting restrictions to be lifted saying that he hoped the publicity might lead to someone identifying what he described as 'the real killers'.

'Mr Harvey is the last person in the world that she would deliberately have killed,' he said.

When the magistrates agreed that Tracie should be granted bail so that she could spend Christmas with Carla, the prosecution argued there was a risk she might attempt suicide again. Robinson said the police efforts to find witnesses were substandard and that Tracie's overdose shouldn't be seen as an act of guilt because she regretted it and was determined to clear her name.

Thankfully, Robinson's efforts failed and Tracie ended up being taken to Eastwood Park Women's Prison in Gloucester.

'That'll give the bitch a taster of what's in store for her,' said Ray, when Mick came and told us what had happened.

It felt good to know Tracie was banged up inside that weekend and was hopefully getting to know a reception committee of prison inmates.

But on the Monday, the day before Christmas Eve, a judge at Oxford Crown Court decided Tracie should be released on bail, dismissing the CPS argument that she might have another go at killing herself. The only condition of her bail was that she stayed with Irene and Alan.

It was sickening to watch her crying and hiding her face with her arms as she and Robinson were filmed outside the prison. 'My client is overwhelmed by the events of the past few days,' he said. 'She's very pleased to be going home and to her freedom.'

As if that wasn't bad enough, he said the publicity of her court appearance had prompted a witness to come forward. A significant witness, he insisted.

Ian Johnston assured us that he knew nothing about anyone coming forward and that, whatever Tim Robinson thought he had up his sleeve, nothing would interfere with the police investigation.

The police were amazed she'd been freed. They told us how unusual it was for anyone facing a murder charge to await trial on bail but the CPS had to go along with the judge's decision. We were outraged. It meant Tracie was in a far better position than most criminals who get banged up on remand for far less serious offences. Not just because she had her freedom, but it would also give her defence team access to her whenever they wanted without having to go through the usual prison-visiting formalities. She'd have all the time she needed to prepare her case and rehearse her performance in court.

The only good thing about her release was the fact that the media besieged her mum's house. Reporters told us the roads outside Irene's house were full of camera crews and photographers trying to get a glimpse of her. One photographer had even climbed on to Irene's garage to try to get a picture of Tracie having a fag in the back garden.

We guessed it would take more than that to make her crack. There was too much riding on the trial for her to start losing her rag in public. She was certainly being put under pressure, although it didn't seem to stop her going out with her friends in the evenings. A friend even told us that they'd seen her drinking in the pub over the road from our hair salon one evening. Maybe if I hadn't had the self-control and restraint in those early months before the trial, I'd have gone and given her a good slap.

But we knew we had to show some dignity. Tracie could down as many of her favourite Malibu and pineapples as she liked and pick up as many men as she wanted but she was still a murder suspect.

It was hard not to believe the stories that Lee's mates told us about her. One or two of them said they'd walked out of a pub in disgust after she showed up on another bloke's arm. Another of his mates from work found out that she'd even had sex with a bloke she'd met way before Lee and he'd promised her a modelling job. 'They got this agreement,' he said. 'He gives her 50 quid every time he takes some photos of her and she lets him shag her.'

It was a bad time for all of us. Ray was still signed off work from his lorry-driving job with stress and we were both really worried about Michelle and how she was coping with her pregnancy. Steve was a rock for her, helping out with Paige and the housework while Anita was doing her best to comfort Danielle.

When I wasn't at the salon, I visited Lee at the hospital chapel every day. It really helped to sit alone, talking to him. Spiritually, I felt so close to him and the physical presence alone was comforting. It made me feel peaceful, calm.

Michelle and I worked at the salon until lunchtime on Christmas Eve. It was hard but we couldn't let the clients down and we felt that we had to try to prove to ourselves that we could endure a normality of sorts. Everyone was so kind, bringing us presents of wine and flowers and going out of their way not to mention their own family celebrations at a time when we were dreading the thought of not having Lee with us.

In the afternoon, I went to see Lee. We'd never spent a Christmas apart and I didn't want this one to be any different.

As for Christmas, well, we had to put on a brave face for Paige and Danielle but, despite the carol singers at the door, we didn't have the heart to put up a Christmas tree or decorations. It had been heartbreaking enough to see another sympathy card in the post in the midst of so many others covered in snowmen, angels and glitter, let alone to think about making the effort to buy the usual goodies and presents.

There were so many memories of the Christmas Days we'd shared when Lee and Michelle were younger, especially the year when Ray and I bought Lee a Mini after he'd passed his driving test. I'd taught Lee to drive. He was a natural and could hardly wait for our lessons together. After six weeks, I told him I thought he was ready for some professional lessons with the BSM.

He passed his test first time and we were so proud of him. The only problem was that I hardly saw my car after that because Lee was always borrowing it. My mum had come over to stay for Christmas that year and, after we'd all exchanged presents in the morning, Ray asked Lee if he'd get him a glass of orange juice.

Even though Michelle had far more presents than him – jewellery, perfume, clothes and even a hi-fi, dear old Lee hadn't moaned once as he opened boring old socks and jumpers. He loved Christmas. Just being with Danielle, watching her squeals of delight as she opened her presents and spending the day with his family was all he ever wanted.

87

We were all grinning at each other as we heard him rooting around the fridge looking for the orange. 'Go and have a look in the garage,' I said to him. 'I think I've put some out there.'

We all piled into the kitchen as he went out through the back door. His face was a picture when he saw the gleaming red Mini with a huge red bow tied to the windscreen with a card saying 'Merry Christmas, Lee'.

'Oh, Mum, Dad, Nan... Is it really mine?' he shouted, hugging us.

It was the best Christmas ever.

Lee loved his Mini. It was the first of many that he used to buy and loved doing up to sell on. He was always buying bits and bobs for it – new mats, bucket racing seats and alloy wheels. The twin exhaust he fitted made such a racket that I used to put the kettle on as soon as I heard it coming up the road.

Christmas was also a time to remember my mum. She'd died on Christmas Day in 1989 within a few weeks of being diagnosed with lung cancer. She was only 66 and I felt cheated that she'd been taken from me at such a relatively young age.

With Lee, the shock and sense of loss was far worse. Like all parents, Ray and I had never expected to outlive our child, let alone lose him in such nightmarish circumstances.

The lights went out for us that year. And it was hard to imagine that, without Lee, they'd ever come back on again.

He and Tracie had been Christmas shopping for their girls in November. Danielle wanted her Tiny and Tim twin dolls and Lee had wanted to make sure he got them early in case the shops sold out. Tracie had bought her some books and a Polly Pocket castle.

When the police came round with the presents before Christmas which they'd found in Tracie's flat, our first instinct was to refuse them. We didn't want anything from her but decided that, because it was Lee's last gift to Danielle, we had to accept the presents for her sake.

My sister Barbara, bless her, invited us all to go to her house for Christmas Day. It was a wonderful gesture, which, initially, we refused because we didn't think we'd be able to face it. We'd even thought about staying in bed for the day until it was all over. We were in such a state that we couldn't contemplate the idea of socialising and knowing that the conversation would inevitably turn to Lee and Tracie.

'It'll do you good,' Barbara said, when I told her about our plans to stay at home. 'If it gets too much, you can leave whenever you want to.'

We knew she was right. We had to make the effort to get out of the house and knew that Barbara, her husband Derek and their two boys Christopher and Ian would make us all feel welcome, so we agreed to go.

First thing on Christmas Day, we all went to the chapel to see Lee, and from there to the cemetery to lay flowers on our mums' graves.

At the Robin Hood Crematorium in Olton, we laid red roses on the plot we'd bought for Lee and then toasted him with a glass of brandy.

Everything seemed so bleak, so surreal. In so many ways, it was the opposite of Christmas.

9

Tears for Lee

On Boxing Day, when I phoned the hospital to tell them I wanted to spend some time with him in the chapel as usual, I was stunned to discover he'd been moved to a temporary mortuary in Birmingham. Tracie's legal team had contacted the Crown Prosecution Service to say they were considering carrying out a second post mortem on him as part of their defence enquiries.

The police told us there was nothing we could do to stop it. It was devastating news. I cried for most of the day and then drank a bottle of brandy with Ray.

I couldn't stop thinking what sort of a time Tracie was having with her family. Our family and friends were being so supportive but Ray and I just wanted it all to be over. The only thing that kept me going was the hope that this was going to be Tracie's last Christmas at home.

On 5 February, two days before Lee's funeral, Tim

Robinson called a press conference. The police phoned, full of apologies, to say that, although they hadn't been invited, they would be attending to find out what Robinson was planning to say.

When we watched it on the television, we thought how bizarre the whole thing seemed. Robinson said that Tracie's road-rage story had been corroborated by three new witnesses, one of whom claimed to have heard two cars driving at speed past his house near Cooper's Hill. Tracie, Robinson said, would not be making a statement but he would be releasing more information at a later date.

That day, I didn't give a damn about Tracie Andrews or her solicitor. I knew it would be the last time I would see Lee. The undertakers had advised me not to, but I knew heaven and hell would have to freeze over before they stopped me. I'd given them a designer shirt to dress him in for the funeral. I knew Lee would have loved it but, when I saw him in his coffin for the first and last time, it felt like someone had hit me with a brick. Not because of the way he looked – Lee was still my son despite the fact that he'd been lying in a refrigeration unit for nine weeks – but because I knew this was going to be the last time I'd ever see him. I know from speaking to other grieving parents that what I felt that day was perfectly normal, in the sense of wanting to cling to the most precious thing in your world. Or as normal as you feel knowing they're never coming back.

Michelle didn't want to see her brother. It was just too much for her to bear but she waited in another room while I said my goodbyes. It was a moment when I mentally played back Lee's life in a few minutes. The memory of that intensely powerful feeling of pure love that I'd felt holding him for the first time when he was born. Of seeing him as a smiling little baby with his arms outstretched in his cot, kissing his knee as a toddler and wiping the tears from his big brown eyes when he'd fallen over. Remembering him posing proudly in his uniform as Ray took his photograph on his first day at school. Riding his bike, bouncing on our bed, snuggling into my arms when I kissed him goodnight.

So many cuddles, kisses, smiles. So much happiness. As a parent, you lock those special moments away in your heart forever. I just thank God that Ray and I had those wonderful times with Lee as he grew up and became the man we'd always been so proud of. Tracie Andrews had taken his life, but she would never destroy our love for him.

More than 350 people turned up to pay their respects at Lee's funeral on 7 February. His mates from West Midlands Travel arrived at St Nicholas's Church in King's Norton in a number-35 single-decker bus. It was the service that Lee used to drive and there was even a huge photograph of him on the front. His best mates Adam, Mark, Adrian, Barry, Graham and Trevor were pallbearers. It was heartbreaking to think that Lee wouldn't be around to share so many wonderful events in their lives in the future.

As Ray, Michelle, Steve and Anita followed Lee's coffin from the hearse, it seemed unimaginable that we had come to say goodbye to our son at the same church where he and Tracie had planned to marry in four months' time. Even Michelle and Steve had been married here in May 1996. The memories had always been so happy.

At our request, the police had told Tracie to stay away and that, if she or anyone from her family turned up, they wouldn't be welcome. Maybe she was frightened or maybe she simply summoned up her last ounce of good grace but she took their advice. She'd meant nothing to us when Lee had been alive; she meant even less now he was dead.

Our wonderful friend Eve Pitts, the minister who had helped us plan the funeral, kept us strong that day. We had baptised Lee at St Nicholas's in 1972 so she knew how much it meant to us when we'd asked her to officiate at the ceremony. Without her, we would never have been able to find the strength even to take those first faltering steps into the church.

Thank you, Eve, for everything. You will be in our hearts until the day we join Lee in heaven.

It was a beautiful service, even though, as Eve said, it was a day that none of us would ever have imagined, not even in our darkest nightmares. 'This is an unimagined nightmare,' she said. 'A policeman knocks at Maureen and Ray's door with a message no parents want to hear, a message that Lee's life has been cut short by a murderous act. If the love which everybody felt for Lee could have brought him back, this would have happened.'

She told the congregation that she was speaking not simply as a priest, but as a human being and a mother. 'This service is meant not just as a service to say goodbye but to give all the thanks we can muster to say thank you for Lee's life, albeit a short one. He was a much-loved son, father, brother, workmate, school friend and, today, all of us grieve for his untimely death. But I pray and trust that what we are thinking about today in our grief must not overwhelm us. We must recall the years of happiness which Lee brought to so many.

'Lee was a bright, mischievous boy. At school, he always rushed his work, finished before the other members of the class and then insisted on helping other pupils – whether they wanted help or not. Everyone who knew him respected him. As a man, he packed 50 years into his 25. He loved life; he loved karate, snooker and golf. He never followed the crowd. What he wore was his own style. His presence lit up the room wherever he was.'

Standing at the front of the church, Michelle broke down in tears, as she explained how her life would never be the same without Lee. 'I love him so much,' she said, 'but our loss is God's gain and heaven will now be a much brighter place.'

It was heartbreaking to see our beautiful daughter wiping her eyes as she took her seat again. She was having to hold her own family together while watching Ray and I crumble and fall apart.

My brother Alan read some of the words from 'Call the Man' by Celine Dion, which he'd told us had given him and Babs comfort after Spencer's death. It was yet another poignant moment as he shared them with us.

Alan knew only too well what Ray and I were thinking as we watched Lee's mates carry his coffin out of the church. One of the saddest memories I have of that day was the sight of Danielle's white roses spelling out the word 'DAD' in the window of the hearse. We'd agreed that going to Lee's funeral would be far too much for Danielle, so her other granddad arranged a trip to the zoo instead.

She had written the words on the little card herself: 'To Dad. Have a wonderful day in heaven. Love and miss you, Danielle, xxx.'

Michelle's card on her flowers said simply: 'Thanks for being my brother.'

None of us could hold back the tears as we watched Lee's coffin being placed inside the hearse. It was draped with a scarf and a flag in the blue-and-white colours of his beloved Birmingham City Football Club.

It had been a day we'd all been dreading and I still don't know how we got through it. We were still facing so much uncertainty, so much heartache. We wouldn't be able to lay our son to rest until the woman he had loved and trusted was brought to justice.

On 19 February, there was another bizarre twist in Tracie's defence team's efforts to undermine the police investigation into Lee's death. Tim Robinson released a photo-fit of the alleged road-rage killer – a man who he claimed was named 'Jez' and had been behind another road-rage attack on a company chairman. In his press release, Robinson said he had a signed statement from the wealthy businessman who had been attacked in the same area as Tracie and Lee.

According to him, Jez, who had been driving a Ford Sierra, had produced a knife and threatened to cut the man's throat during a confrontation near the Marlbrook pub. Jez had the same overweight, staring-eyed appearance as the passenger of the car who Tracie said had killed Lee and had threatened him at around 6.00pm on the same evening as Lee's death.

'A dangerous psychopathic knifeman is still at large in the Birmingham area,' Robinson said dramatically. 'A man who is greatly respected was driving his car near the Marlbrook pub when there was a minor road-rage incident.'

When Brian saw the video-fit that Tracie had drawn up with a firm in London, he couldn't get over how much it looked like him. Even his mum thought so. Brian was the first police officer who Tracie saw after Lee's death and he was her liaison officer. We thought the whole thing smacked of desperation; so did the police. Tracie hadn't managed to do a photo-fit at the time of Lee's death because she'd said it had been too dark to get a good look at his attacker. And yet, nearly three months later, she'd come up with a clear picture of the man who, if Robinson was to be believed, was still running round Birmingham brandishing a knife.

If the press and public needed any sign from the police that this new move was simply a diversion tactic, it was evident in their deafening silence. 'West Mercia Police declined to comment,' it said at the end of the regional media reports about Robinson's photo-fit plea.

We knew the police weren't taking Robinson's so-called witness breakthrough seriously but it still rankled to know that he and Tracie were doing their best to protest her innocence before the trial. It seemed that, every time we turned on the television or opened a newspaper, there was a story about Tracie appearing in court on remand or trying to worm her way out of her bail conditions.

On 27 March, the police told us Robinson had successfully applied to Worcester Crown Court for a variation of Tracie's bail conditions. I'd just got home from the cemetery. Sometimes, it was comforting to stand by the grave and remember the good times. Other times, like that day, I'd been sorting out my fresh flowers in the rain and I'd heard someone screaming.

They were crying so bitterly it made my chest pound and stopped me in my tracks. Whoever it was, it sounded like they were in pain and the sound of their anguished sobs were getting louder and louder. I looked round expecting to see a woman at another grave but there was no one there. It was *me*. The sound of screams and crying had come from me and then, suddenly, I felt someone's arms around me. It was a woman and she'd heard me crying. She wrapped her arms around me and looked at me with tears in her own eyes.

'Come on, don't cry like this. He wouldn't want you to,' she said.

I don't know how long I stood there in the driving rain by Lee's grave, sobbing in this woman's arms. She didn't say anything else but just held me. I never saw her again but I felt so much better as I drove home. A stranger who just happened to be there when I needed someone.

The news about Tracie's bail conditions was the last thing I needed to hear.

'She wants to go on holiday to Bournemouth for a week with her family,' Brian told us.

We were disgusted. We couldn't afford to go on holiday. We'd spent our savings on Lee's funeral and yet the person accused of killing him was able just to pack her case and go and enjoy herself. It seemed as though she was being allowed to do just what the hell she liked and yet, even when we wrote to our MP Julie Kirkbride complaining, we were told there was nothing we could do because, like anyone accused but not found guilty, she had her rights. She could go out and get drunk, breach the hours of her curfew, go off to the sodding seaside, go shopping with her mum.

It didn't take long for the newspapers to pick up on the story of how she'd had sex with a married man whom she met at the holiday camp. Stylish stuff, as it always was with Tracie. She spots Mr Tight T-shirt across a smoky bar, asks him to buy her a Malibu and then pops round to someone's caravan for a shag. And just to make sure he didn't change his mind when he found out she was a murder suspect, she'd even given him a false name, calling herself Tina.

We weren't surprised when the police had told us she was going to plead not guilty. We knew Tracie too well. She wasn't the type to go down without a fight. And we knew she'd get Robinson to pull out all the stops, try every trick in the book to convince the jury that she was innocent.

Every time we went to court at Redditch Magistrates, Tracie looked more at ease but still clearly irritated in the dock. It was almost as if she was using her remand appearances as rehearsals for the press attention she knew she'd get at her trial. We knew that, once she'd been committed, it would go quiet, until there was a date set for her to appear at Birmingham Crown Court.

There were two people who stepped in to help us through the weeks that followed who we will always cherish as special friends. In May 1996, Ken and Toni Cameron had lost their son Stephen in a brutal road-rage attack on the M25 near their home in Swanley, Kent. Stephen, who was just 21 and about to set up his own electrical engineering company, died protecting his fiancée Danielle after a motorist in a Land Rover cut up their van on the motorway slip road. Ken saw the paramedics fighting to save Stephen as he lay dying in the road. He'd said he'd only needed to take one look at his son to know that it was hopeless. Stephen had been stabbed twice, once fatally in the heart. An unprovoked attack on an innocent young lad with his whole life in front of him.

When his mum and dad saw the news of Lee's death, they asked the police if they would put us in touch with them in the hope that we could help each other. The first time they phoned us, we talked for almost four hours. We all cried, not just because we made ourselves relive so many memories about our children, but because it was such a relief to speak to people who knew what we were going through.

Our hearts went out to Ken and Toni. Even though a year had gone by since Stephen's death, the police were no nearer to catching his killer. It would be another three years before an Old Bailey judge would sentence Kenneth Noye to life imprisonment for his murder.

When Tracie was charged with Lee's murder, it didn't change the bond between us all. If anything, it brought us even closer together, even though, at the time, the police investigating Stephen's death hadn't charged a suspect. We, of course, were convinced that the police had got Lee's killer, but were still trying to come to terms with the fact that she had not only taken our son, but had betrayed us as well.

The most chilling aspect of us all meeting was the fact that we'd told the police about the comments Tracie had made while watching the news of Stephen's death on the television news. Road-rage incidents at the time weren't ten a penny then like they are now. And, because Stephen's death was the first of its kind to happen during such a confrontation, it became an extremely high-profile case. Tracie blaming Lee's death on a road-rage attacker was for us, and the police, no coincidence after what she'd known had happened to Stephen.

Toni told us that working as a nurse meant she'd seen more than her fair share of suffering. But, even knowing and working with people who'd lost a loved one, she had never realised the enormity of grief. Unless it's your child or children, you can never put yourself in their place.

'I just never knew it would be this bad,' she told me. 'There seems to be something eating away inside me. An empty, raw pain. I don't think it's ever going to go away. I feel so guilty about being alive. I would have died to save my son.'

Ray and I knew exactly where they were coming from. Even Danielle, who had been with Stephen since the age of 14, felt guilty that she hadn't been able to stop his attacker. The guilt, the sadness, the emptiness were part of the bond we had.

It helped to know that both our boys had packed in so much in such a short time. They seemed to have had so much in common – football, golf and always being up for a good time. We all felt that, if they'd met in another world, they'd have been good friends.

When things became too hard for Ray and me to bear during those months leading up to the trial, the weekends we spent with Ken, Toni and Danielle were unbelievably comforting. Even though it's a friendship that came from such tragedy, it will always be very special to us.

10

The Trial

We didn't get much sleep the night before the start of Tracie's trial on 1 July 1997 at Birmingham Crown Court. The kettle went on at 5.00am and Ray and I sat drinking tea until DI Walters, Mick and Brian arrived to pick us up at 7.30am.

'You can pose for photographs on the court steps but don't say anything to the reporters,' Steve told us. 'There's a room reserved for you at court so you won't have to worry about bumping into Tracie's family. The next four weeks isn't going to be easy for you but you're going to get through this.'

We knew Steve was right but we still felt sick with nerves. The thought of being in the same building, let alone the same room, as Tracie turned my stomach.

But she was the one on trial, not us. We'd waited seven months for this day and, despite Tim Robinson's efforts to disparage the police investigation and the fact that no murder weapon had been found, we just hoped that the forensic evidence was heavily stacked against Tracie. For Lee's sake, as much as ours, the jury had to see through her lies and give us the guilty verdict we were praying for.

'If only Lee was the one going into the dock for murder instead of Tracie,' Ray said on the way to court.

It was something we'd both agreed on almost immediately after realising Tracie was the main suspect. We'd wanted it to have been her funeral, not Lee's. We'd have given anything to have him with us, even if it had meant him facing a murder conviction and the prospect of a life sentence, we'd have been able to see him in prison and wait for him to serve his time.

We were surrounded by photographers on the court steps when a people carrier pulled up and Tracie stepped out with Irene, Alan and Tim Robinson. As the photographers rushed down the steps, she flicked back her hair, licked her lips and stood smiling at the flashlights exploding around her.

In the two-and-a-half years that we'd known her, never once had we seen Tracie in a blouse buttoned up to the neck; she'd always made sure her cleavage was permanently on show by wearing skimpy little tops that barely covered her. And yet, here she was, demurely done up in a pin-striped trouser suit looking more like a cross between a school ma'am and a CID officer. If this was the moment she'd been waiting for, then she was bloody well welcome to it; we had no intention of hanging around to watch.

Inside the court, we were briefed on the format of the proceedings and then, after yet more tea, were finally shown to our seats in Court Nine. Irene, Alan and Tracie's younger sister Donna came in with their family supporters after us and took their seats behind us.

The press benches and public gallery were packed and, with people queuing to get in, my brother Alan, sisters Barbara and Josie, Ray's sisters Audrey and Betty and Anita took it in turns to sit with us in our little room when the judge retired.

Many of Lee's mates had wanted to be there but ended up taking it in turns to queue. Even though we didn't get to see much of them, it was so comforting to know they were rooting for us.

Ray and I were so proud of Michelle. She didn't deserve to be sitting in a courtroom just a month after giving birth. She should have been at home, trying to settle into a routine with a new baby. In the months leading up to the trial and the weeks after it started, she was so brave and supportive for me and her dad. Like us, she and Steve were going through hell, always trying to put on a brave face and telling us not to worry. But they were there for us, every step of the way. Just as they are now, ten years later. However blessed Ray and I felt by the gift of little Jordan when he was born, his mum and dad were just as heaven sent.

Any thoughts we'd had of using the court café to snatch a sandwich sailed out of the window when we saw Tracie and her family sitting round a table. It was as if they were out on a day trip, laughing loudly and joking, as they kept turning round to look at us. We felt far less intimidated in our little room. It was crowded with all of us crammed round a tiny table but at least we didn't have to watch Tracie swanning up and down in the foyer.

David Crigman, the prosecuting QC, said Lee and Tracie had gone through a string of violent bust-ups in the two-and-a-half years that they had been together. 'This was a pair who sometimes lived together and sometimes lived apart, depending on how much they were arguing,' he said. 'When the turbulence of their relationship became too much, Lee would move out and go back to his parents.'

He then described a row which had started at Tracie's flat six weeks before Lee's death when she'd told police that he'd thrown a video cassette at her. 'She was upset,' he said. 'Telephone equipment had been broken and she complained this had been done by Lee in the course of an argument earlier that evening. There was a television on the floor which she said had been dropped by him in an argument between them the night before.'

He also mentioned another nightclub argument which had been so fierce that other clubbers had gathered to watch them. 'Later that same night, in the early hours, they were seen arguing in a lay-by by two police officers in a patrol car,' he said. 'A week after that, police were again called to the defendant's flat after a neighbour heard them rowing and the deceased was packing his clothes. The evidence shows that they both participated and the crucial significance is to underline the turbulent and explosive nature of their relationship.'

Mr Crigman said that, even on the day of Lee's death, the

neighbour living above Tracie's flat had heard them arguing. 'Even the neighbour's hard-of-hearing mother-in-law had heard raised voices before and during their Sunday lunch,' he added. But he said they had made it up, gone to the Marlbrook pub and had then driven home.

'It is the prosecution case that during that journey their volatile relationship again exploded and a fierce, violent argument broke out. Although other drinkers in the Marlbrook pub had noticed an air of unease between them, the argument would have started in the car. It led to the car being stopped and both of them getting out. When they were out of the car, the defendant launched the most vicious attack on Lee Harvey using a penknife blade from an imitation Swiss Army knife.

'The ferocity of the attack on the boyfriend and the area where the attack was concentrated, namely the neck, would quickly have rendered Lee Harvey defenceless. Both the carotid artery and the jugular vein were severed. It would have led to the immediate and massive spurting of blood pouring from his neck. No doubt he would have tried to move away from her but he could not have moved far before collapsing on the ground and dying. It is likely that the attack continued after he collapsed and abated only after her anger had subsided.

'After the attack, she was to claim that the death was caused by the occupants of another car during a driving dispute. The evidence shows unequivocally there never was another car, there never was some mystery murdering motorist... it was her.

'At the time, she was seen as a potential witness but, with

hindsight, her activities at the hospital where she was taken to be treated for facial injuries – inflicted by Mr Harvey in their final and fatal confrontation – may provide an explanation of how she disposed of the knife. She was allowed to go to the toilet alone and a long time passed. A nursing sister became worried and knocked on the door. Andrews said she was all right and emerged.

'During the three hours she spent at the hospital, she returned to that toilet several times. The plastic bin inside the lavatory's waste bin was emptied, unchecked, hours later and its contents passed into the rubbish-disposal system.'

Mr Crigman said that, although the knife hadn't been found, DNA tests on the inside of Tracie's boot revealed a 2.5-inch by 1-inch bloodstain. Blood, he said, that was a mix of Tracie's and Lee's. 'There is extremely strong evidence to support the view that Andrews tucked the knife inside her boot,' he added.

Mr Crigman said that a witness, Richard Main, who had been visiting Keeper's Cottage, left just after 10.45pm and heard a woman calling for help and requesting an ambulance.

'Was she tending the body of the man? No, she was not,' he said. 'Was she running to the house for help? No, she was not doing that either. She was standing by the driver's door with her back to the car and she was covered in blood. The defendant made no mention of Lee having been stabbed by a pursuing motorist and Mr Main did not hear another car speeding away.'

He added that bloodstains found at the scene did not

match Tracie's version of events. 'Lee was attacked and bleeding in a wholly different location from that where the defendant claims he was attacked. Parts of the knife, a pair of bloodstained tweezers and the spring from a pair of scissors were discovered near Lee's body. They had broken off from the murder weapon due to the ferocity of the attack,' he said. 'The hand which held the knife would also have been cut. Andrews's right little finger was found to be lacerated when she was examined by a doctor.'

He also described how a clump of almost 100 hairs from Tracie's head, mostly still with the roots attached, had been found on the left sleeve of her leather jacket. Three other strands of her hair were found in Lee's hand. There was also blood found on the back seat of Lee's car, which was inconsistent with the account that Tracie had given to the police. And blood on her orange jumper suggested it was splashed on rather than from cuddling Lee.

For the first time since losing Lee, we were no longer in the dark about what had happened to him. It was horrendous to think that Tracie had gone to such lengths to try to save her neck. The thought of her shoving the knife in her boot while Lee was dead or dying in the road in front of her and then covering up her plan to get rid of it at the hospital with crocodile tears was too horrible to take in.

All I could think of that evening at home, as Ray, Michelle and Steve sat talking about what Mr Crigman had told the court, was what a bloody fool I'd been to go along with her bullshit. The haunting image in my mind as I fell asleep in the early hours was of me and Tracie holding hands at the press conference. I'd held her right hand...

the hand in which she'd held the knife that had ended Lee's life.

Every morning during the trial, Steve, Mick and Brian would turn up at the house at 7.30am to collect us. The routine was the same every day. Once we'd been photographed and followed by reporters on the court steps, we'd dive straight into the court to avoid the mass bun fight that followed Tracie's arrival.

Sometimes we'd get sandwiches from a little bakery near the court and stay in our room to eat them, other times we'd enjoy the sunshine in the grounds of St Phillip's Church. The fresh air was always welcome, but, if we did sit on the public benches, we were always watched from a distance by a photographer or a reporter. Strangers would often come up to us and say how sorry they were about Lee. At least a dozen of them told us they hoped Tracie would pay with a life sentence for what she'd done to him. Not one person came and told us they hoped Tracie would be acquitted.

Despite going out of our way to avoid Tracie and her family in the court foyer, there were still times when we were forced to watch her laughing and joking with them. Throwing back her head and shaking her hair, it was almost as if she knew we'd be watching. It's one of the most frustrating parts of any trial. As well as going through all the grief of bereavement, you might have to put up with living in the same area or facing intimidation from relatives, so the last thing you need when you finally get to court is to face the defendant, their family and supporters.

110

I suppose Tracie's family had to put on a show and pretend they weren't worried because they probably knew the clock was for ticking for her. The police didn't waste any time telling them to keep out of our faces when we complained and, after the first week, they disappeared into one of the witness rooms.

There was one occasion when Alan Carter bumped into Ray in the toilets. He made the mistake of trying to speak to him and Ray told him in no uncertain terms to stay away from him. 'If you know what's best for you, you'll just keep out of my way,' Ray had said. 'Not just for today, but for the rest of your life.'

When the trial wound up for the day, the police would often take us for a drink on the way home. They didn't have to do it, but it really helped us. We had nothing to go home for apart from sitting and going over and over the evidence we'd heard.

The only laugh we had was joking about Tracie's outfits. One day she'd be in pinstripes, the next day she'd fiddle with the gold buttons on a power jacket that looked as though it had come straight off the set of *Desperate Housewives*. Sometimes, the look would be Miss Jean Brodie meets Miss Marple; other days she looked like one of those American TV trailer-trash mums who end up cat-fighting with their husband's girlfriend in front of a studio audience. It was the only light relief we could rely on at the time. We knew Lee would have found it funny.

We were worn out but still unable to sleep at night. If I didn't have a bath, I'd stand in the shower for ages with the radio turned up loud. With the hot water cascading down my face, the tears would come easily and, at least, I was on my own and no one could hear me. Or so I thought.

Michelle told me a few weeks later, after the trial was over, that they'd all heard me sobbing. 'It doesn't matter, Mum,' she said. 'You'd go mad if you didn't have a good cry. We all do it.'

The next day, we heard evidence from two people who were in Baker's nightclub in Birmingham on the night Tracie bit Lee's neck and punched him. Stephen Girling, one of Lee's best mates who'd gone out with him that evening, and barmaid Victoria Silcock, said there had been a heated argument between Tracie and Lee after Lee had turned up at the club.

'Tracie was shouting at him because she was angry he'd come to the club,' said Victoria Silcock. 'I saw her punch him twice on the cheek – the punches were hard enough to make him flinch but he didn't retaliate – and then bite him on the left side of the neck and scratch his chin. Lee was taken to the kitchen because the bite was bleeding and needed attention.'

Three police officers also gave evidence about fights they'd witnessed between Tracie and Lee. Ian Henderson said he had seen them scuffling outside a pub on Broad Street in Birmingham and that Lee appeared to be trying to calm Tracie down as she tried to hit him. He said he and another officer had been forced to separate them and had then sent Tracie home in a taxi.

Grant Moss said he'd been called out to Tracie's flat where she'd told him they'd had numerous violent arguments, and David Hind said he'd been called to the flat on another occasion to stop them fighting.

'Tracie was in a worked-up state and quite aggressive towards Lee,' he said. 'There were lots of verbal exchanges between them but, when we split them up to talk to them separately, there were constant interruptions from Tracie as she tried to get back into the room where Lee was sitting.' Even when Lee left the flat, he said Tracie was still aggressive towards Lee and shouting at him.

We were delighted that so many independent witnesses had seen Tracie's violence towards Lee and how he'd always tried to defuse her hostile behaviour. We knew exactly what she was like but now, thankfully, so did the jury.

If ever there was a day when Ray, Michelle and I felt the evidence in court was going to provide incontro-vertible proof of Tracie's guilt, it was 3 July. In extracts taken from a 40-minute-long video filmed by the police, we saw for the first time the little girl who lived at Keeper's Cottage and who had been in bed on the night of Lee's death when she heard a row outside. Nine years old and cuddling a teddy bear, Stephanie Duncan said she heard two people arguing – an angry man and another person with a softer voice. 'I know the man wasn't very happy,' she said. 'He sounded quite fierce to the other person. I woke up because I could hear the noise and the curtains were lit up and I could hear some people talking outside. It sounded as if they were arguing, though I didn't hear what they said.'

What Tracie could never have imagined as she stood covered in Lee's blood concocting her cock-and-bull story was that she was about to come face to face with a former CID officer. Stephanie's mum, Susan Duncan, had been a detective constable for West Midlands Police before leaving the force to work as a defence solicitor. She told the jury that she suspected Tracie had killed Lee after speaking to her that night.

As Richard Main, a friend who had been visiting her that evening, left the cottage, an automatic security light came on and he saw Tracie bending over Lee in the road outside. Caught like a rabbit in the headlights, Tracie had only started screaming for help once she realised she'd been spotted. Susan Duncan said she came outside with a mobile phone and a torch when Mr Main told her to ring for an ambulance.

'It was very dark in the lane but I could see a man lying in the road near to a parked car,' she said. 'A blonde woman was standing behind the car. She was distressed and crying. The man wasn't moving and I couldn't hear him making any sounds. There was blood everywhere.'

Ms Duncan said she would definitely have heard the sound of another car speeding away if there had been one. She went on, 'Tracie Andrews told me she had been in the Marlbrook pub and her boyfriend had had an argument with some other men. She told me Lee had cut someone up and that he had stopped his car. She said she had told him not to get out of the car but he did. The next thing she said was, "I put my hand to my face and there was blood everywhere."'

Crucially, Susan Duncan then said that Tracie had claimed to remember nothing about the other vehicle or the appearance of the men Lee had argued with.

'Later, when the police were talking to her in my kitchen, she said it was a black Sierra, that it was the passenger who'd attacked Lee and she gave police a description. After she left my house, I began to suspect her.'

I felt like rushing over to kiss Susan as she left the court. It was damning evidence from someone who was not only an experienced copper but also, luckily for us, had been the first person to speak to Tracie before she'd had a chance to invent her story.

Simon Baker and his girlfriend Elaine Carruthers, who were both accountants, were fantastic when they gave their evidence the next day. Tracie had said that she and Lee had missed their turning while being chased and had had to do a reversing manoeuvre in order to get back on to their route home. Mr Baker said they had seen them travelling in the opposite direction and saw Lee reversing. But he and his girlfriend then drove for about five miles along the same route that Tracie said she and Lee had taken. They had both seen only Lee's car, no others. And certainly not a dark Sierra in hot pursuit.

'I say Miss Andrews' story is completely and utterly untrue,' Mr Baker said. 'I would definitely have noticed another car. From the moment I saw the Escort, there was definitely no sign of a car behind it, unless it was at a distance of five miles behind.'

Police driving expert Brian Seabourne told the court that overtaking was impossible at the spot where Tracie had claimed the Sierra had got past. He said the combined width of the Escort and a Sierra was five inches wider than the lane. 'The driver being overtaken would have to slow or even stop to let a second car pass,' he said.

Joanne Mitchell, a nursing sister at the Alexandra Hospital, described how Tracie had used the toilet, containing a sink and a rubbish bin, six times in just three hours. Within five minutes of her arrival at hospital, Tracie had spent between five and ten minutes in there.

'I knocked on the door and asked her if she was all right,' she said. 'I was worried she might have collapsed. When she came out, I noticed that she had tried to clean herself up.'

Between then and 12.20am, when the police came to take away her clothes and boots as evidence, she had returned alone to the same toilet.

At 1.07am, when she was told Lee was dead, Joanne Mitchell recalled, 'She was sitting on a bed. Her dad was at her side. She pulled off the blanket and asked me why she couldn't cry.'

By the time Tracie was discharged at 2.36am, Sister Mitchell said she had visited the same toilet three more times, saying that she'd been drinking at the pub or was suffering from shock. Mr Crigman said Tracie had thrown the knife in the toilet bin but, by the time police suspected her, it had been emptied.

Audrey May, a domestic supervisor at the hospital said a cleaner would have removed the clinical waste bag from the bin between 7.00am and 8.00am on 2 December. She said it would have been taken without examination to a holding tub and, later the same day, to the hospital incinerators.

On 7 July, hearing pathologist Dr Helen Whitwell's evidence about Lee's post mortem was, without doubt, one of the hardest days of the trial. It was essential to us to know everything about how Lee had died, to find some comfort in the hope that he hadn't suffered. Dr Whitwell said the two wounds at the back of Lee's neck had penetrated through to his skull and another to his chest had left a mark on his breastbone. I watched Tracie wiping her eyes as Dr Whitwell said Lee would quickly have been incapacitated and died of haemorrhaging from multiple stab wounds.

When photographs of Lee's body were produced for the jury to look at, Ray and Michelle got up and walked out of the court. It had been hard enough for all of us to listen to Dr Whitwell's evidence but the photographs were too much for them. It wasn't difficult to see the images from where I was sitting, but I'd promised myself that, however painful it was, I was staying.

It was shocking because, when I'd seen him for the first time in the hospital morgue, I hadn't remembered seeing any of the cuts that covered his face on the scene-of-crime photos. No matter how many times I wiped away the tears that began to roll down my face, I couldn't stop them coming. I felt sick but concentrated on staring at Tracie as she bowed her head to look at the photographs. She was shuffling them like playing cards but, as she went through each image, there were no tears. No emotion. She was looking at Lee's dead body, at the knife wounds *she* had made all over his face, head and neck. Dozens of angry, crimson weals, splattered with blood, raised cuts criss-crossing gaping wounds. I couldn't understand why, as she carefully studied each image, Tracie appeared to be so calm. It was almost as if she was just going through some old holiday snaps.

One of the 30 wounds to his neck had cut his carotid artery and there were a further two wounds to his jugular vein. Dr Whitwell said that, although it was impossible to tell which of them had caused his death and how much force had been used, the one to his chest which had gone through to his breastbone had been 'significant'.

On 9 July, it was the turn of forensic expert David Loxley to give evidence about the bloodstain found in Tracie's boot. He used genuine and imitation Swiss Army knives to demonstrate to the jury how part of the knife, with its blade closed, matched the stain. In his opinion, the stain next to the zip couldn't have been made by blood simply splashing on to the inside of the boot.

Tracie smiled when Ronald Thwaites, the defence barrister, asked David Loxley if it could have come from a bloodstained thumb. 'Miss Andrews could have put the mark there herself taking the boots off, couldn't she?' Thwaites suggested.

Tracie smiled again when Mr Loxley answered, 'If, indeed, her thumb was wet with blood, yes.'

When he was asked to explain the break that appeared in the stain, Mr Loxley explained that the boot could have been folded so the knife wouldn't have touched part of the fabric. 'My view was that there was an overall similarity rather than a detailed agreement between the knife and the fabric,' he added.

The next day, the jury watched a videoed recording of Mick interviewing Tracie. It had been done 18 days after Lee's murder. On the television screen in the court, we watched her staring at the floor as Mick suggested she'd tried to commit suicide because she was guilty about killing Lee. 'I wanted to be with him,' she told him. 'I felt so helpless because you kept going on at me. I feel like a broken person. Like I've got no future. I've lost my boyfriend. If I had done this, trying to get away with it, why would I try to kill myself? My whole life's been turned upside-down. I know it's selfish to take your own life. I said, when I was in hospital, I just wanted to be with him. I could never be with anybody else.

'We've had our arguments and split up a few times, when Lee would go back to his parents' house, but we always got back together again and loved each other. Every night when I go to bed, I really miss him.'

She admitted they'd argued 'about nothing major' on the day of Lee's death and had been talking about Carla and Danielle in the pub. Lee, she said, had made a snide comment about Carla's dad but they hadn't argued. 'I suppose Lee was just jealous that I'd been with another man,' she added.

Mick also asked her why her story didn't coincide with the forensic evidence found at the scene. 'Something had gone on in the car, hadn't it, Tracie?' he asked. 'That's why he pulled up there, and you've gone over the top and then had to come up with a story. If it happened on the spur of the moment, then so be it, but let's get it out. Do you want to tell me about it?

Tracie looked at him, her arms folded and her legs crossed. 'I would rather just speak to my solicitor please,' she said.

That afternoon, Ronald Thwaites said the police had

ignored calls from police informants who, he claimed, had repeatedly identified Tracie's description of Lee's killer. The man, a bouncer referred to as Mr X, had been involved in a road-rage attack several years earlier and had apparently followed Lee out of the pub on the night he'd been killed. Ray clenched his fists and swore under his breath as Thwaites told the court that Lee was a known drug-dealer who knew Mr X.

I couldn't believe what I was hearing. Lee had never been involved in drugs; it just wasn't his scene. Ray and I had lost count of the number of times we'd heard him condemning people who sold drugs for the misery they put users and their families through. It was upsetting to think Tracie's defence team were trying to blacken his name, but we knew the truth. And the jury knew from listening to the post-mortem details that there hadn't been a trace of drugs in his body. Lee had always said that what made him happy was a couple of pints and fags, and a bird was an added bonus. It wasn't much of a bonus for Lee, though, that the bird he ended up with was Tracie.

According to Thwaites, an anonymous caller had phoned the police on 6 December claiming Mr X had been in the pub at the same time as Lee and Tracie. Reading the police logs, he said, 'When Harvey left the pub, he was followed by Mr X, having had long eye contact as Harvey was going. It was thought they were going to fight but Mr X got into the passenger seat of a dark-blue Ford Sierra.'

He also said an officer from the Regional Crime Squad had given Mr X's name on 3 December after receiving a call from an informant. He said Mr X had been carrying a large amount of cocaine in the Marlbrook. His description of a fat man with piercing eyes matched the one that Tracie had given.

'Did you kill Lee Harvey?' It was the first question to Tracie from her defence barrister Ronald Thwaites on 14 July.

'No, I did not,' she said. 'I loved Lee more than anything in the world and I didn't want to live without him.'

It was sickening to watch her standing there looking so smug, leaning on the rail of the witness stand, calmly sipping water and smiling. I gripped Ray's arm when Thwaites commented that she was wearing the engagement ring Lee had given her.

'Yes,' she whispered. 'I was wearing it on the night Lee died.'

We watched as she walked across the courtroom with a female prison guard and held out her ring hand for the jury to see. It was another Oscar-winning performance, as Ray used to say. Lee had bought the ring from Birmingham's Jewellery Quarter. I'd even gone with him and Tracie to help choose the bloody thing. It had been Tracie who'd insisted on my going, even though I'd told her it was something they should do together. The diamond cluster she chose was beautiful but the ring needed altering because it was too big.

That night, Ray and I went out for a celebratory curry with the two of them. Even now, it makes me cringe to think how we all went along with her 'happy family' plan.

'Don't think you're going to get away without proposing to me,' Tracie had told Lee. 'I want you to get down on both knees and ask me properly.'

Lee was happy to oblige because there was hardly anyone in the restaurant but a waiter came running over moments later when Tracie suddenly started screaming.

'Oh my God, there's a stone missing!' she shrieked.

She was the only who couldn't see the funny side as we all got down on our hands and knees to look for it. We never found it but, after polishing off the best part of a bottle of wine to herself, Tracie lightened up.

'Christ, I thought she was going to go off on one in there,' Ray said on the way home.

I knew what he meant. The jeweller had probably loosened the setting when he'd been altering the ring. It was no one's fault but I suspected poor old Lee would be in for an ear bending when they got home. It was sorted out when they took it back the next day but Tracie had chucked the ring at Lee during so many arguments since then it was surprising there were any ruddy diamonds left on it at all.

On 15 July, David Crigman said Tracie had used her experience of another road-rage row she'd had with a former boyfriend to make up her story about Lee's death. Even Irene and Donna looked stunned when he said she'd driven off with the driver of another car on her bonnet after a row near her old home in Alvechurch. Tracie was as cool as a cucumber as she denied the incident and said the driver had confronted her when she drove into the back of his car.

'The lad I was going out with was going to have a word with him,' she said. 'The driver tried to stop me driving away.'

Mr Crigman also suggested that Tracie had chosen an F-registered dark-coloured Ford Sierra in her road-rage story because Lee had previously owned an F-registered Ford Orion. And that she had turned off the headlights on Lee's car to deliberately play for time after killing him to think up a story.

'In your statement, you said the headlights were on but the evidence of the police and the owner of Keeper's Cottage was that the lights were off,' he said. 'Your blood mingled with Lee Harvey's was on the edge of the car door which you had pulled further open to switch off the lights. You wanted it dark for more thinking time. If anybody had looked out, they would have seen the lights.'

When Mr Crigman asked Tracie why, when she was so used to shouting at Lee during their arguments, she had not filled her lungs to bellow for help, she looked at the floor. 'I should have done a lot of things,' she said. 'I suppose I was in shock.'

'What happened that night was that you and Lee had a row,' Mr Crigman contested. 'You both stormed out of the car, to the back of the car and there was an almighty set-to and, during the course of it, you got a penknife and stabbed him time and time again.'

Tracie seemed to have composed herself again as she listened to him. 'I did not,' she said.

When he asked her what she was doing in the minutes that had passed between Lee collapsing and Richard Main seeing her, she said, 'I don't know. Everything was just like a dream. Lee was lying on the road. I didn't want to leave him. I can't explain why I didn't sound the alarm. I was in shock myself. Nobody knows what they would do in that situation.'

Mr Crigman then pointed out that she would have been the sole eyewitness to Lee's attack. Why would the mystery killer have left her at the scene?

'To be honest with you, I wish hc had killed me as well so I wouldn't have to stand here,' Tracie said.

'From what you've said, Lee would have been moving from the rear of the car towards the front to his attacker,' went on Mr Crigman. 'A truer version of events would be that you followed him brandishing the knife as he desperately tried to retreat. If he'd taken knife wounds to his neck and back that were bleeding so seriously as to cause splashes of blood on the floor, he'd retreat, wouldn't he? It is a path of retreat, isn't it? He's going to try and get away from whoever is sticking a knife into him again and again. You are the only person in this world who can account for what happened that night and it was you sticking your knife into him as he retreated from the back of the car to the front.'

Tracie glared at him. 'No, I did not,' she said. 'How many more times can I explain? I did not see it. I knelt down by Lee's side and I had my arm underneath him. I was in a really bad way myself.'

'And the hair,' demanded Mr Crigman. 'How do you explain the clump of your hair being found?'

Tracie raked her hand through her hair and looked at the jury. 'The only explanation I can give is that Lee held on to me at some time.'

I cried when Mr Crigman mentioned the hair. Hearing that it had been found in Lee's hand, I couldn't put the image of him trying to defend himself from Tracie out of my mind – clawing wildly for survival while she was repeatedly plunging a knife into him; stabbing him over and over again as he fought to try to save his life.

When Ronald Thwaites opened his defence on 17 July, he seemed determined to convince the court that the frequent rows between them were Lee's fault. 'The prosecution say the defendant had a motive for murder. She says she had a motive for marriage,' he said. 'This is the man she had fixed upon to spend the rest of her life with. They had glamour with each other, charm with each other. They wanted each other. She was wearing his ring on the night he died and is wearing it still today. She was committed to him.'

Mr Thwaites described Tracie as sensible, level-headed and practical. She was, he said, a young woman who coped with her life as a single mother. 'By contrast,' he said, 'Lee Harvey was a person who could not cope very well with his life. He bitterly resented paying maintenance to the mother of his young daughter which was one of the reasons why he gave up his job so that the CSA couldn't get money from his employers.'

It was sickening to listen to his character assassination of Lee. He'd always looked after Danielle financially, as we had and still do. And the only reason he'd packed up bus driving was because he'd wanted to find a better-paid job. One of his friends who worked for Birmingham City Council had helped him get a job there. Like us, Tracie knew the truth. The only reason he hadn't managed to start it was because she'd killed him.

The police had warned us before the trial started that if

we made any comments or interrupted the proceedings then the judge would have no alternative but to order us out of the court. It was the last thing we wanted after waiting so long to see Tracie in the dock but it was hard to sit behind her family, watching them shake their heads and whisper to each other. It was sickening for us to have to sit so close to Tracie but at least we could watch her every move. And even though she wouldn't look at me, she knew that, if she dropped her guard and glanced my way, I was there, right by her side, just as I'd been at the press conference before she'd been charged.

The only time I lost my composure was listening to Mr Thwaites's opening remarks. Ironically, my outburst caused Tracie to lose hers. Nothing could ever have prepared us for hearing her admit that she'd lied about something that had caused us a great deal of heartache, and made us feel an enormous amount of sympathy for Tracie at the time. In November 1995, we thought she had suffered a miscarriage. Now, for the first time, we were hearing the truth about what had really happened. Throughout the whole unfortunate episode, we had been led to believe that she'd fallen down some steps while out shopping. It was now being revealed that she'd booked herself into a clinic and had an abortion.

In that split-second, I could remember every detail as if it were yesterday – Tracie and Lee coming home to tell us they were going to have a baby... Lee being over the moon at the prospect of becoming a dad again.

What bloody fools we'd been to believe her lies. She'd sat there, pretending to cry as Lee had wept in my arms, while

I'd told him that there was no reason why they couldn't have a baby in the future. Tracie hadn't only murdered Lee, she'd murdered his baby.

Just as I was thinking what a blessing it was that Lee had been spared the awful truth, Mr Thwaites delivered a further shocking blow in the courtroom. Tracie, he said, had admitted to Lee what she'd done during a row while they were on holiday in Portugal with Danielle.

The thought that Lee had known what she'd done but had saved us from finding out was too much to take in. Knowing how upset Ray and I would have been, and what we would have said to Tracie had we known, he'd protected us. He hadn't even told us that he'd gone ahead and paid for her breast enlargement a few months later, another fact that emerged while Mr Crigman was going through the details of Tracie's medical records.

'Lying bitch,' I muttered under my breath.

Tracie swung round to look at the public gallery where Ray, Michelle and I were sitting. 'I want her out of this court,' she snarled. 'I won't put up with this while I'm giving evidence.' The simpering, doe-eyed look on her face had vanished. Instead, it was twisted with anger, her eyes blazing as she glared at us from the dock. Ronald Thwaites said he hadn't heard any remarks but said anyone making comments in the public gallery would be ejected. The judge agreed but said he hadn't heard anything but thought he'd heard me cough or cry. Thank you, I thought.

Tracie's outburst hadn't done her any favours. The jury was seeing her true colours; I'd won this round.

When she was asked to explain the blood mark in her

boot, Tracie seemed a bit more composed. 'I have no explanation at all,' she said. 'I was covered in blood and kneeling in blood but certainly I didn't have anything in my boot. I have done absolutely nothing at all.'

He also brought up the details of a black woolly hat which he said Tracie had planted at the roadside in the hope that the police would think it belonged to Lee's attacker. Tracie claimed she'd never seen the hat before in her life. Strange then, Mr Crigman told her, that a forensic examination on it had revealed hairs on it that had matched her mum's cat. Ray and I had been asked if Lee owned or had ever worn a black woolly hat by Brian Russell when he took our statements but we'd said no. It just wouldn't have been his style.

He was like a dog with a bone when he asked Tracie to explain the time difference between Lee's death and Richard Main leaving Keeper's Cottage. She'd claimed the attack lasted ten minutes, he said, yet the evidence proved that it was 17 minutes before Richard spotted her. Why, he wanted to know, hadn't she sounded the car horn or run to the cottage for help?

'I was in shock,' she whispered. 'I didn't want to leave him.'

'With a man with whom you have a relationship lying immobile on the floor?' insisted Mr Crigman. 'You don't even shout to the house, let alone go to it?'

Tracie chewed her lip and glanced at the jury. 'No, I did not,' she said.

'What you wanted outside that house when you'd come to the shocking realisation of what you'd done was some thinking time, wasn't it?' he asked her.

'No!' shouted Tracie.

'And the nine-year-old girl who lived at the house and heard what she thought was an argument between only two people?'

'She was wrong,' said Tracie.

'When could you have got blood that came out in a gush like a fountain from Lee's carotid artery on your jumper?'

Tracie tried to look composed but I could see she was trembling. Was it rage or fear? 'I can't answer that,' she said. 'I don't know.'

She gave the same answer when Mr Crigman asked her to explain how her hair came to be found in Lee's hand.

When Mr Crigman showed the jury a Swiss Army penknife similar to the one that had been used on Lee and said it would have cut the attacker's little finger if it had been closed, she stared straight ahead. 'You suffered a similar wound, didn't you?' he asked her.

Tracie said nothing.

Later, she said she'd changed the story she'd told the police because she was so traumatised at having to retrace the route of the car chase. 'If someone had said there was a pink elephant there, I would have agreed,' she said.

Mr Crigman smiled at the jury and then at Tracie. 'You didn't go as far as pink elephants but you've invented a black Sierra, haven't you?' he said.

I'd seen the look of utter contempt that she shot back at him a thousand times before. The defiance and anger in her face was unmistakable. 'No,' she said.

There was another fantastic twist to the trial the next day. Fantastic for us, but not for Tracie. Key defence witness Stephen Rodenhurst was revealed to be a convicted criminal who had served prison sentences for a number of offences. He'd been arrested and brought to court after refusing to testify but then told the jury he'd been involved in a road-rage incident on the same day as Lee's murder a few miles away. He claimed his turbo-charged Bentley was tailgated along the A38 past the Marlbrook pub by a dark-red Ford Granada at 5.00pm. The car had then pulled up alongside his and the driver, whom he described as a lunatic, threatened him with a knife after an argument.

He said he'd contacted Tim Robinson after seeing the photo-fit of the fat staring-eyed attacker whom Tracie claimed had attacked Lee. The man, he said, looked like the one who'd pulled a knife on him.

It was a wonderful moment for us when Mr Crigman told the jury about his criminal past. He had a record dating back to 1979. A fine 'highly respected businessman' he'd turned out to be.

11

The Verdict

After four weeks of listening to all the evidence, we were back in Court Nine for the last time on Tuesday, 29 July. It was the week that Lee and Tracie had planned for their wedding the following Saturday.

My heart was thumping and I could hardly breathe as I sat next to Ray watching the jury file in. After five hours, they'd reached a unanimous verdict. Nine men and three women who had listened to every detail of the final hours of Lee's life and who were now, God willing, going to bring his killer to justice.

When the foreman stood up and said the word 'guilty', I thought I was going to scream out loud. Ray, Michelle, Steve and I hugged each other as the tears rolled down our faces. The relief was so overwhelming that I had to make a conscious effort to keep breathing.

No matter how composed Tracie was so obviously trying to appear, I could see the shock on her face. The muscles around her jaw flexed as she leaned forward to steady herself against the rail of the dock. Her cream summer coat and customary four-and-a-half-inch heels were the perfect going-away outfit. Only where she was going, the dress code wouldn't require such glamour.

Before Mr Justice Buckley passed sentence, Thwaites stood up to deliver his mitigation. When he referred to Tracie's 'lack of courage to confront her own wrongdoing', it was the first clue we'd had about what appeared to be his personal take on the case. The police had told us that he'd asked Tracie to consider pleading guilty to a manslaughter charge which doesn't carry the same mandatory sentence as murder. Thankfully, she had refused to play ball and now it was too late.

'Had she explained what happened, the outcome might have been different,' Thwaites said. 'But she stands convicted of murder. The court may wish to believe that this killing was the result of a spontaneous outburst of passion mixed with other powerful feelings which she converted into deadly actions. Lee Harvey has lost his life, the life of this woman is in ruins... she has a daughter of just seven. If Miss Andrews could put the clock back, she would dearly love to do so.

'It is a case that arises out of tragic domestic circumstances. Perhaps the temperaments of the two people were wrong for each other. They were too similar. They enjoyed and endured a love-hate relationship that culminated in this tragedy.'

Whatever Tracie was thinking, her face gave nothing away as Mr Justice Buckley then began his sentencing.

'The jury has found you guilty on very strong evidence of murder,' he told her. 'Only you know precisely what went on that night but we have all seen the awful consequences. Certainly, it has been a tragedy for all concerned and I feel deeply for the families on both sides. There is only one sentence prescribed under law and that is life.'

At that moment, I said a silent prayer for Lee. Thank you, God... look after my precious son until I can be with him. Let Lee finally rest in peace.

Behind us, we could hear the stifled sobs and gasps from Tracie's family. Irene and Tracie's sister Donna were crying in their seats behind ours. Donna hadn't looked at us once during the trial, even though there had been a couple of times when we'd caught each other's eye as she'd repeatedly handed notes to Tracie's defence team. It felt good to know that the next time she'd see her twisted evil bitch of a sister would be across the visitor's table in a prison.

As the judge stood up to leave the courtroom, she and Irene left. They couldn't get out of their seats fast enough, their heads bowed, as they pushed past the family members sitting near them.

I'm sure no one would have cared if we'd jumped up and down and shouted 'Yes!' but we didn't. We wanted to maintain our dignity and, instead, sat together hugging each other and wiping our eyes.

It was pandemonium when we stepped into the foyer outside the courtroom. The police, Lee's friends and our family rushed over to hug us and shake our hands. Reporters who had sat through the trial in the press benches came over to hug us, congratulating us on Tracie's sentence. Yes, we were delighted that we'd finally seen justice done for Lee but it was a hollow victory of sorts. Nothing, not even Tracie's life sentence, was going to bring him back. We'd wanted justice so badly that I don't think anyone in our family really believed that she'd get off. But, knowing that you can never count your chickens, it wasn't something we'd dared to consider.

The police had asked us not to say too much to the media outside the court because they had organised a press conference at Steelhouse Lane Police Station in Birmingham city centre. They told us Tracie was hysterical in the court cell. The Ice Maiden, as she was described in a TV documentary a few months later, was in such a furious state of meltdown that a police doctor had been called to sedate her. Irene and Alan, Thwaites and Tim Robinson had only been allowed to stay with her for a few moments.

It felt good to know that she was suffering like us. After months of carrying on her life as if nothing had happened, holding her head high for the cameras, deluding herself that the jury would believe her lies, her day of reckoning had finally arrived.

Ray was in floods of tears but managed to compose himself before we walked out of court. I was bursting with joy and, even as we stood together on the steps being photographed, I had to stop myself leaping up and down.

Ray only acknowledged one reporter, Mike Kilbane from the BBC's *Midlands Today*. Out of all the reporters whom we'd met, he was the one whom we both felt had shown us the most kindness and understanding. Ray told him that it wasn't a day for celebration; there were no winners, only justice for Lee and a chance for us finally to lay our son to rest.

Tracie's dad John and her brother Lee had already left the court without speaking to the press as Tim Robinson came out and produced a prepared statement:

> *We're very surprised by the verdict. Miss Andrews is devastated by it, as are her family. I've seen my client and she is conducting herself with great personal dignity as she has done throughout the case, but she finds it hard to believe she is in this position. There will be an appeal but the grounds have not yet been decided. Miss Andrews has been convicted of murder, an offence she has vehemently denied and which is based largely on circumstantial evidence.*

His words were laughable. Since when did hysterical screaming constitute great personal dignity or irrefutable forensic evidence become circumstantial?

At the press conference that morning, Steve Walters read out a joint statement which he'd prepared with Ian Johnston. West Mercia Police had told us there was bound to be an inevitable line of media questioning about the way they'd conducted such a high-profile investigation. Why, maybe, Tracie hadn't been arrested earlier on and why no one on the team had pre-empted her suicide bid in the face of the witness accounts which had come to light three days after Lee's death.

Knowing he'd be the one taking any flak, Ian Johnston had taken annual leave and gone on holiday to avoid any criticism. But, in the statement, he'd made it crystal clear that the police initially had no reason to doubt Tracie's road-rage story. It was only after receiving witness statements from the couple in the car who'd seen Lee's car travelling towards Cooper's Hill that Tracie had become a suspect. 'Those people both saw Lee's car at the time and place in question,' said Steve. 'Their description of the manoeuvres it carried out was accurate. Yet at the time they did not see any trace of a dark Ford Sierra as seen by Andrews, which caused us to question her version of events.

'I believe she and Lee were two people who could not live together but who could not live without each other. There were frequent arguments and outbreaks of violence between them. But, while Lee's anger was always directed towards property, Andrews did, on occasions, carry out physical attacks on him. I believe Andrews is a young woman who was trying to make a life for herself but who suffered many setbacks along the way. She was unable to make a relationship with the father of her child and her life was obviously extremely difficult. There was a great deal of jealousy on both sides but they kept being drawn together.

'I can't say whether the overdose she took was a result of remorse for what she'd done or whether she could not face life without Lee. But, when she went into hospital, it simply gave us more time to follow up new lines of enquiry.'

The police had three exhibits, which had been shown to the jurors during the trial, on display for journalists and photographers to look at during the press conference: Tracie's tangerine-coloured, crushed-velvet polo-neck jumper, heavily marked with blood down both sleeves and

bove left: This was Lee's favourite bike. It originally belonged to his play school but
loved it so much that we exchanged it for the brand new bike we had just given him.
other kids couldn't believe it!

bove right: Lee and I were really close. Here we are on a family holiday when Lee was
urteen years old.

low: On holiday again, this time at Butlins when Lee was younger. That's us on the
ht, proudly holding our prize for second place.

Happier times. *Above*: Lee and me with my brothers, Kevin and Alan.

Below left: Ray and I on a Royal Caribbean Cruise in April 1995, before tragedy struck our family. You can see how happy and carefree we were …

Below right: The happy faces in this picture masked so much disharmony and pain. Here are Lee and Tracie at Christmas in 1995. By the following Christmas, he had been taken from us.

ove: A family snap that became public property. This picture was used alongside
ss reports of the case.

ow: I can't come to terms with the fact that we welcomed Tracie into our home and
family.

Above: The Marlbrook pub, where Tracie and Lee were drinking on the night of his murder.

Below: Lee's car, the one he was driving that night.

bove: The blood-stained jumper that Tracie was wearing when she killed Lee.

low: I still find it hard to look at this picture today; it was taken at the press nference when we appealed for any witnesses to come forward. Although Ray had doubts, at first I stood by Tracie and wanted to believe her version of events.

Above left: The blood-stained boot in which Tracie hid the knife.

Above right: Ray and I arriving at Birmingham Crown Court, hoping that justice would be served.

Below: The Andrews family outside the court. Tracie's mother Irene is on the right and stepfather Alan on the left. On the far right is Donna, Tracie's sister.

Ray and I have taken great comfort and support from our friendship with Ken and Toni Cameron, the parents of Stephen Cameron; Stephen was murdered in a road rage incident. *Top*: A day out with Ken and Toni. My brother Alan is pictured far right.

Above left: Ray gets ready for a game of golf with Alan and Ken Cameron.

Above right: Toni and I busying ourselves in the kitchen.

Left: We originally campaigned to bring back capital punishment but it was Jack Straw who suggested we campaign for a life sentence to mean life. *From left to right*: my daughter Michelle, Ray, Jack Straw, me and Julie Kirkbride, our MP.

We cherish every
single memory of Lee.

the front; the patent-leather, mock-crocodile-skin ankle boot where she'd hidden the blade she'd stabbed Lee with; and a Swiss Army-style knife similar to the one she'd stabbed Lee with.

For Ray and me, the press conference was a chance to finally vent our anger, to let the world know how Tracie had broken our hearts with her lies. We also now had an opportunity to ensure that she and her family were under no illusion about our feelings of contempt towards her.

'We feel nothing but hatred for Tracie Andrews,' said Ray. 'We will never be able to forgive her for taking the most precious thing in our lives. Life in prison is the only option in this country but we'd prefer capital punishment by lethal injection for something as serious as this where it has been proven and all the evidence is against her. She shouldn't be kept in a three-star hotel, but that's effectively what prison will be like for her.'

Ray said that Lee had been held in the highest regard by everyone who had known him and that the only problems he'd ever had to deal with in his life involved Tracie. 'Our son was wonderful,' he said. 'He had an aura about him. When he came into a room, it was as if he had brought a light with him.'

I explained that the only reason I'd supported Tracie at the witness appeal press conference was because I'd wanted to give her the benefit of the doubt for Lee's sake. 'We took her into our home and tried to like her,' I said. 'Michelle and Ray both thought she'd done it when we heard about Lee but I gave her a chance because I wanted to believe she loved him. Ninety-five per cent of me felt she was guilty, but the other 5 per cent I held back because of Lee. He worshipped her... trusted her. I desperately wanted to believe my son had died in his lover's arms, not by his lover's hands. But, as the trial went on, the evidence became stronger and I knew in my heart of hearts she was guilty. It's been one long nightmare. We have all been to hell and back.

'Tracie Andrews has taken Lee's life and sent him to heaven prematurely, but we've been sent to hell for the rest of our lives. I hope that every day she takes breath she remembers what she has done. I hate her. If we had capital punishment, I would happily administer a lethal injection to her myself.'

It was the first of many interviews we gave to the press after the trial in which we opened our hearts about our feelings towards Tracie. Despite all the speculation and intrusion, with journalists digging away trying to find out what had made Lee and Tracie tick, there was never a time that Ray and I felt the media weren't on our side. Of course, we weren't stupid enough not to realise that Tracie and her lies were the reason why the case was so high profile. She was perfect lady-killer material. The bleached-blonde hair, the make-up that looked as if it had been applied with a brickie's trowel and the break-neck shoes she'd worn to teeter up and down the court steps every day were trademark accessories.

And, however sickened we were by her theatrical performances in the dock, we knew that, simply by looking as though she'd stepped straight out of the pages of a third-rate magazine, she'd always guarantee herself a place in the next day's papers. If not to fuel the fantasies of their male readers, then to warn their wives and partners that inside a minority of good-time girls there was, potentially, a psychotic bunny-boiler just waiting to get out. The world had heard her story without having had a chance to hear Lee's.

It was this, more than anything, that made it so easy for Ray and me to give interviews and appear on the television, especially after having had to keep quiet for so long and not prejudice the trial. We wanted anyone who was prepared to listen to know exactly what Tracie Andrews was really like.

The following day, as we appeared on *GMTV*, the world woke up to front-page headlines about Tracie's life sentence and TV footage of the white prison van speeding away from the court. We already knew Tracie had been preparing for a guilty verdict after speaking to Rod Chaytor, the reporter who had covered the case for the *Daily Mirror*. There was no doubt in our minds that Tracie had anticipated a guilty verdict when we read Rod Chaytor's report. He'd been the only journalist at the witness appeal press conference who had unnerved her with his questions about timing discrepancies. And yet, desperately wanting a last chance to declare her innocence publicly, she'd given him an exclusive interview in one of the courtrooms moments before the jury returned its verdict. And, ever the opportunist, she'd even handed him a poem which she'd written about Lee.

The headline said it all: LYING TO THE END – EVIL TRACIE PLAYS THE INNOCENT AS SHE GETS LIFE JAIL SENTENCE. And Chaytor had had a field day with her comments, branding her a liar and describing how, despite being minutes from a life sentence, she had clung to the hope that she'd got away with murdering Lee. However sickening it was to read, it proved she was incapable of expressing any remorse and defiantly believed she, not Lee, was the victim.

'Of course I loved Lee,' she'd said. 'I still do. No, I didn't kill him. I know they are going to find me guilty of murder but I didn't commit this terrible crime.'

Chaytor had described how she'd puffed on a cigarette and fiddled with her engagement ring before giving him the poem which the *Mirror* had published in full. Entitled 'Goodbye, My Love', it was rambling childlike nonsense about how much she missed Lee:

> *My love is so deep, in my thoughts are you I keep,*
> *Your eyes are still shining, your voice I hear.*
> *The pain is intense to not have you near.*
> *I want to be with you to feel the feel,*
> *That we have shared in body and soul.*

The thought of Tracie sitting at her mum's kitchen table with a fag burning as she sat writing such a load of old shit was almost as ridiculous as her efforts to try and win public sympathy. She'd never written Lee a poem while he'd been alive – why dedicate this Mills and Boon-style bollocks to him now?

'I watched him die and part of me died with him,' she'd said. 'I'm not responsible for his death. I know I'm going to prison but I'll fight to clear my name.'

Her plan to make people think what a caring, sensitive

soul she was had backfired, though, because the paper had left its readers in no doubt about her guilt.

Another headline story to emerge that day was Andy Tilston's. He hadn't made a police statement or given evidence at the trial, but he'd happily spoken to a reporter. It would have been a lot harder to cope with if we hadn't heard it from the horse's mouth. But, when we saw the story splashed across two pages in all its tabloid glory, we couldn't understand why Andy had done it. It was his sensational account of how Tracie had threatened him with a knife after a night out at a working men's club near her home.

'I'd only had one drink but Tracie lost her temper about me wanting to drive home,' he'd said. 'When we got home, she flipped. She took a knife from the kitchen and waved it towards me. She'd lost it. I took the knife from her hand and grabbed her. When Tracie gets angry, her eyes go wide.'

Andy said that, when police had interviewed her about the incident, she'd claimed he'd driven home drunk and denied ever having grabbed the knife.

The sex sessions that had kept Lee going back to Tracie were mirrored in the three-month relationship she'd reportedly had with Martin Lismore. He'd talked to another paper, saying that he'd ditched her after recognising what he described as 'inner rage' and felt lucky to have got out of the relationship. His revelations about their sex life left nothing to the imagination as he described their all-night bonking sessions. 'She'd do anything to please her man,' he said. 'She was bloody good in bed. Very adventurous and demanding. She needed it every day. She was a nymphomaniac. She couldn't get enough. She had all the gear to turn me on... She would start on me while I was sitting in the chair and spend half-an-hour caressing me to get me in the mood. Then we'd go to bed and make love for a couple of hours. The minute I woke up in the morning, she'd start on me again. She'd always have music on while we were in bed. Once, when we went out together, she flicked up her black dress to show me she wasn't wearing any knickers. She was so sexually demanding I couldn't keep up.'

Lismore said that one night, after he'd fallen asleep after yet another marathon sex session, Tracie had woken him up wanting more. 'I obviously went along with it for a bit but it wasn't going anywhere for me so I got out of bed,' he said. 'I made the excuse I was going to work and she snapped, "That's nice, you get me all turned on and then you just fuck off." I was surprised by the sudden change in her. Seeing the unpleasant side of her character helped me to decide to finish with her. I didn't like what I saw. In the light of what happened to Lee, I'm so glad I did.'

Reading Martin's account of his relationship with Tracie was like déjà vu. She'd displayed the same controlling behaviour that we'd seen when she was with Lee. And, just as she'd been so jealous of Lee's platonic relationship with Anita, Tracie had even suspected Lismore was trying to rekindle his relationship with the mother of his children. Just as she'd stalked Lee, she'd followed Lismore to his ex's house when he called in to see his children one day and then asked him why he'd been to see her. 'She made it very clear she had her eye on me and that I wasn't going to get away with anything on the side,' Lismore said. 'I knew it would never last because she was so possessive and only seemed interested in settling down. That was no good for me. She was the kind of girl you'd like to see a couple of times a week for ever, but that just wasn't on.'

When he finally ditched Tracie, he'd even admitted taking flowers and a letter round to her flat when she wasn't in. 'When I next saw her out on the town, she flashed a V-sign at me and was very angry,' he said. 'But, when I saw her again some time later, she came over all smiles and said she was getting married. She promised to invite me to the wedding.'

It was nice to think that Irene and Alan would be reading the same reports as us, especially Lismore's description of how Tracie liked to play the Meatloaf song 'Bat out of Hell' while they were having sex.

'More like "Bitch out of Hell",' I said to Ray. 'Christ, it even says here that she decorated her bedroom in black with matching cupboards and duvet.'

In another story, engineer Richard Morgan said he'd almost died beneath the wheels of Tracie's car after she smashed into his parked car late one night. David Crigman had mentioned the incident during the trial, describing it as a road-rage attack which she'd used to make up her story about Lee's fictitious attackers. Richard Morgan said he'd leaped on to the bonnet of Tracie's car to avoid being mown down as she drove straight at him five years earlier in December 1991. She'd been travelling at 30mph and had even swerved the car to try to shake him off as he clung to the windscreen wipers.

'I'll never forget the hatred on her face as she stared

through the windscreen,' he said. 'She showed no mercy. She didn't care if I lived or died – all she wanted was to escape without being caught. I was virtually on top of the bonnet, thumping the windscreen, but she began to go faster and faster. I was skating backwards with my feet scraping under the bumper. If my heels had caught I'd have been pulled straight under.'

Even after police had traced Tracie's car and her insurers had paid up £300 for the damage to Richard's Maestro, he was summonsed to appear in court charged with damaging her wipers. The case was dropped after the truth emerged about her driving off after hitting his car.

Even Greg Collett, the guy who, thanks to Tracie's lies about a mystery fat man, became a prime suspect in the inquiry, had talked to the press. He'd been named as Lee's killer in no less than five calls to the murder team and, because his dad drove a Sierra, he was pulled in for questioning before Tracie's arrest. He described Tracie as a 'lying, malicious, evil, conniving bitch' for trying to put him away for Lee's death.

In two separate reports, carried in *The Times* and the *Scotsman*, we were sickened to read that Tracie had been at a family party in Irene's back garden the night before her conviction. A neighbour living near Irene's said that, although it had been Irene's birthday, the family had seen it as a joint celebration because they were so confident of an acquittal. Irene, the neighbour claimed, had even said it was only going to be a matter of time before Tracie was back home for good.

It was gut-churning to think that so many people had

been inviting reporters into their homes to talk about their links with Tracie while we'd been going through such a stressful time. But you can't reinvent the wheel where human nature's concerned. Murder trials sell newspapers and, at the end of the day, the media coverage of Lee's death had helped to put Tracie behind bars. We'd have felt differently if someone had been critical of Lee but we knew he'd had a skeleton-free cupboard. Tracie had done her level best to blacken his character with her lies during the trial, but now she'd just spent the first night of her life sentence at Risley Women's Prison for her trouble.

The only issue that Ray wanted to redress was the suggestion by Tracie's defence team during the trial that Lee had taken drugs. And he dealt with that during the *GMTV* interview by saying that Lee had never taken them, and that the toxicology tests taken during his post mortem had proved that.

Ray and I met Tony Blair as were leaving *GMTV*. Looking back, I think we were both so relieved that we'd got through our first interview for a national television programme that meeting the Prime Minster didn't seem particularly nerve-wracking. He'd been following Tracie's trial and seemed sympathetic, if not a little distracted, when we told him we really wanted life to mean life. He'd got an interview of his own to do, so it was hardly the ideal time to do our campaigning on behalf of victims. But he did say that, if ever we needed to contact him, he'd try to help.

12

The Aftermath

The days after the sentencing were a lot harder to cope with than we'd expected. Having had the trial hanging over our heads, we were physically and emotionally wrung out. And, because we'd channelled so much energy into turning up to court every day and sitting through all the evidence, I don't think any of us really knew what to do with ourselves. When people called round, we wanted to be alone. When we were alone, the reality of knowing everyone expected us to start getting on with our lives was overwhelming.

People talk about closure without really understanding what it means to suddenly wake up and realise that this is about as good as life is going to get after losing your child. There is no closure. You don't just move on. You can't. And time doesn't bloody well heal. It might make things a lot less raw, but the pain doesn't go away just because someone's been locked up.

Ray, Michelle and I had had our lives turned upside down. We'd opened our hearts to the media and had shared every intimate detail of Lee's life with Tracie and our lives coping with it. Yes, it was our choice and, when I look back at the piles of press cuttings about Lee's death, I'd say we did the right thing to talk about it.

Before we lost Lee, we'd always been a fiercely private family. We'd never needed to talk to anyone outside our own relatives and close circle of friends about what went on in our everyday lives. Tracie Andrews changed all that. From the moment the police knocked at our door to tell us Lee had been murdered, we became public property. And, like all families who suddenly find themselves in the shadow of a killer, we had to get our heads around the idea that there was no escaping the inevitable glare of the publicity machine that accompanies it. The photograph Ray and I still have on top of the telly in our sitting room is one that everyone who comes into our home recognises because it appeared on television and newspapers all over the world. Even now, someone will turn up to fit a carpet or deliver a parcel and, within a few minutes, the penny drops.

'Was your son killed by that road-rage murderer?' It's a question Ray and I have been asked dozens of time. You don't get used to it, you just put up with it. People are naturally curious, almost casual in their interrogation and, if they're local, then they happily tell you they know a friend of a friend who was once in a bar with Tracie Andrews. Or their aunty's cousin's stepsister used to go to school with her. Like I say, you get used to it. If you didn't laugh, you'd bloody well cry.

When we saw the *Daily Mirror* the next day, we discovered that those who'd spoken to the newspapers about Tracie's past life weren't the only ones talking. Her arrival at Risley Remand Centre – once dubbed 'Grisly Risley' because of its notoriety for sex attacks and drug dealing – had prompted someone else to dish the dirt. An unnamed source said that, within hours of arriving at the jail, Tracie had declared she was more famous than Princess Diana. 'She could have meant it as a joke to mask her real feelings,' they said, 'but the impression it gave was that she was a real hard case who enjoyed all the attention she was receiving. If she thinks she's going to be Queen Bee inside, she'd better think again. Prison can be very harsh and some of the women in places like Risley have been around a bit and can certainly handle themselves. They won't take kindly to someone like Andrews thinking she's better than the rest.'

We knew Tracie wouldn't give a damn about what the other inmates thought of her. Self-preservation would be at the top of her personal prison agenda and she'd probably already worked out that her notoriety as a convicted killer would be her greatest asset. With her sights set on her appeal, she wouldn't be stupid enough to try to square up to any inmate who thought she might need taking down a peg or two.

But she would most definitely want to be the top dog – or bitch, perhaps – and establish her reputation as an inmate who wasn't going to be pushed around. She'd bide her time, butter up the prison officers and then gradually, one by one, pick off the weaker inmates before using her crocodile charm on the tougher ones. As an accomplished actress and a compulsive liar, Tracie's predatory instincts would serve her well on the inside. We just hoped it would only be a matter of time before she met her match. Maybe another killer, whose shared disregard for life would make her a threat, someone who would make sure that Tracie never stopped looking over her shoulder.

That weekend, when we saw the Sunday papers, there was another shock in store for us. The headline in the *News of the World* was the most sensational one we'd seen: I HAD SEX WITH KILLER TRACIE, THEN SHE STABBED ME IN A FRENZY.

Enter Danny Herbert, a nightclub boss who had been waiting in the wings for the trial to end before revealing how Tracie had cheated on Lee with him and stabbed him with a car key. 'That woman was a filth monster,' he said. 'The sex lasted for no longer than 15 minutes but what she wanted to do in that time was sordid and disgusting. I've never met anyone as depraved as her.'

Ray and I were stunned to read that Danny's 'hammer-and-tongs' sex session with Tracie in the back of his car had apparently taken place six months before Lee's murder. Like Lee, he said he'd met her in Baker's nightclub during a dance-night promotion, bought her a bottle of champagne and then took her outside expecting sex in the back of his car. 'There wasn't much room but Tracie was very dominant,' he said. 'Halfway through, she asked me to do something to her that I would never even contemplate. It was just frenzied sex. I didn't even know her name. I had no intention of seeing her again when she asked me for my number, but Tracie went berserk, screaming and shouting that I'd used her. I thought she was a nutter and just wanted her out of the car. I opened the door and told her to get out. I had my back to her at the time.

'It all happened in a second. I heard the jangle of car keys and then felt a searing pain in my back. She'd stabbed me with a car key. I knew she was a psycho and I knew she killed Lee Harvey. She deserves to rot in hell.'

13

Picking up the Pieces

A couple of weeks after the trial, we had two days of phone calls from someone who would hang up when I answered the phone. At first, when I dialled 1471 to find out who it was, the number was withheld. But, when the phone rang a few hours later and still no one answered, I dialled the recall number and heard Tracie's number on the call log.

I felt sick. Why would someone be ringing me from Tracie's flat? Was someone playing a stupid joke on us? My hands were trembling as I dialled Tracie's number and heard a man's voice on the line.

'Who is this?' I asked.

There was a pause. Then the man said, 'I live here.'

I couldn't believe what I was hearing. Had someone broken into the flat and decided to have a laugh at our expense?

'You've got to be joking,' I told him. 'This is Maureen Harvey. Why do you keep telephoning me?'

'Yeah, I know who you are,' he replied. 'Tracie's innocent. And, just so you know, she is going to appeal.'

I hung up on him. I didn't need to hear any more. No one could intimidate us after what that bitch had put us through.

When the phone kept ringing that week and no one was on the line, I decided to tell the police. He made sure he withheld his number so I had no way of proving who it was. The police advised us to change our number; we've been ex-directory ever since.

It was hard when they brought us the clothes and personal belongings that Lee had kept at Tracie's flat. I sat for ages with them in my arms crying. Burying my face in his shirts, stroking jumpers and running my hands over the stitching on his jeans. I couldn't bear to think that Tracie might have touched his things. She wouldn't give a damn what happened to them now. It was a deeply emotional moment, one that I needed to deal with on my own. I'm sure it's something every bereaved mum and dad goes through. There's something very comforting but, at the same time, desperately sad about holding clothes that have been worn by your baby. Yes, I know Lee was 25 when he died, but he'd always been my baby. And I still felt the same about him after his death. You find yourself weeping as you inhale the fading fragrance of a favourite soap or aftershave; staring into space with the comb in your hands that you've found tucked into a jacket pocket; examining the print on an old receipt or a long-forgotten slip of paper or crying into a discarded old hanky. They're all reminders of a past life, things to go on the 'all that's left' pile of the person you loved.

Even now, I can still open the wardrobe door in Lee's old

room and smell his aftershave. It's comforting for all of us, especially Danielle. She loves to potter around his room when she comes to stay. Light and sunny and peaceful, it's a room where any of us can spend a few quiet moments on our own when we want to feel close to Lee. We use it as a box room now. There's not much room but it doesn't stop us all squashing in there, lying on his bed, sitting or standing to use the computer. Lee would have a good laugh if he saw us all in there.

I can remember when Michelle left home; Ray and I asked him if he'd like to move into her room because it was bigger. We thought he'd enjoy having more space for his things but he moved back into his old room after a week.

Looking at his photo albums and touching all his things have helped Danielle to feel close to him. She loves me to tell her stories about when Lee was a young boy and hear how, when she was born, her dad had been there with Anita to see her come into the world for the first time. I tell her how proud he was of her and how he loved her to bits.

It upset Michelle to see Lee's clothes. The one thing her brother had always taken pride in was the way he dressed. Everything he wore had to have a designer label on it. He wouldn't let anyone touch his hair other than Michelle. She was the only one, he'd always said, who knew how to cut it in the style he liked. If he had a hair out of place once he was ready for a night out on the town, then he wasn't happy. Looking the part really mattered to him.

'You're not going to give away his things, are you, Mum?' Michelle had asked when she saw me folding the clothes into a bag. 'They're all we've got left of him.'

It was Ray who had made me realise there was no sense in keeping so much of his stuff. What was the point, he'd wanted to know, in washing and carefully pressing so many clothes and then keeping them in a wardrobe when someone else would be grateful for them? I knew he was right. Lee would always do someone a good turn if he could and I knew he'd like the idea of his things going to someone who wasn't as lucky as he'd been. But the idea of seeing someone in the street wearing a shirt or a jacket that I'd recognise as Lee's just wasn't an option. It would have been far too upsetting, so I knew we couldn't give them to a local charity shop.

At that time, Alan, my brother had booked a holiday in Kenya and said he'd be more than happy to take Lee's stuff with him and donate it to needy youngsters. But, as I took things off the hangers and folded them into a black bag, Michelle kept taking things back out.

She hugged one of Lee's shirts close to her and began to cry as I wrapped her in my arms. 'I know,' I said, wiping the tears from her eyes. 'It's hard, but Lee loved helping people. He'd be really chuffed to know someone else was getting as much pleasure out of all this stuff as he did. Why don't we let Al take half of this stuff and give the rest away when you feel ready?'

We felt better after having a good cry and polishing off two pots of tea. Why is it that things somehow always seem better once you've had a cuppa?

When the police told us we could have Lee's car back, we didn't know what to do with it at first. Michelle was in bits when she saw it in our garage for the first time and Ray couldn't bring himself to go anywhere near it after he'd parked it in there.

156

'Oh God, Mum,' Michelle wept. 'Just think how much Lee loved this car... and now he's dead.'

Even though it had been meticulously cleaned after the forensics team had worked on it, Michelle still managed to find traces of blood on the back seat.

One day, I found Danielle sitting in the front passenger seat, staring into space. I crept back out of the garage when I saw her. I didn't want her to think I was spying on her or that she was going to get into trouble. It was just another way of trying to recreate the closeness she'd had with her daddy.

There was no point in keeping it. It had far too many bad memories associated with it, so we decided to ask the dealer whom Lee had bought it from if he'd sell it. He was shocked because, like everyone in the area, he'd followed Tracie's trial and knew what had happened to Lee, but he said he'd do his best. 'A car's just a car, after all,' he said cheerfully, obviously trying to make us feel better.

I don't think it made much more than a few hundred but the money came in handy when we took Danielle away for a break.

On 15 September, we finally had something to smile about when we read the newspapers. Tracie's solicitor Tim Robinson had spent the weekend in a police cell in Gloucestershire after being arrested by fraud investigators over allegations of misuse of public funds. He'd been released on bail without being charged and, hilariously for us, there was a quote from his wife Bin in one of the papers saying that he'd phoned her on his way home and wanted a hot bath and a glass of wine waiting for him. We were staggered to read that his law firm offices had been raided by the police investigating Legal Aid fraud back in January 1995.

Now, joy of joys, he was being questioned in connection with allegations of aiding and abetting false accounting in his former law firm Robinson and Co and for conspiracy to defraud. It didn't get any better than this after how we'd felt watching his televised performances on Tracie's behalf. Only time would tell whether or not he'd end up facing charges, but it was still nice to imagine him sitting in a police call wracking his brains for the name of a good solicitor.

On 20 September, the day when we should have been celebrating Lee's 26th birthday, Michelle and Steve had Jordan christened at St Nicholas's Church. It was our way of bringing happiness to a very sad day; a time to reflect on what we'd all lost but also to remind us what we'd gained from having baby Jordan in our lives.

After everything we'd been through, we felt that his arrival into the world had been heaven sent to strengthen our hope in a brighter future together. He was 14 months old and such a happy little chap, guaranteed to melt your heart and light up the room with his smile. Just like Lee had done.

Michelle was such a fantastic mum, Steve was in his element as the doting dad and Paige couldn't get over the fact that she finally had the little brother she'd longed for. Their little family was complete.

We held a family party at the rugby club in King's Heath. Naturally, Jordan was the star of the show with Paige and Danielle proudly taking it in turns to hold him. Several of the police crime squad whom we'd met through the investigation joined us for a drink, along with Susan

Duncan, the ex-policewoman who'd given evidence against Tracie. She brought her little girl Stephanie.

We knew from what Susan had told the court that Stephanie's involvement with the case had had a deeply traumatic effect on her and she felt it might help her if she met us. We soon put her at her ease, telling her what a brave little girl she'd been to tell the court what she had heard that night.

The sight of her dancing at the christening with Paige and Danielle and playing mum to Jordan as she wheeled him round in his pushchair is one I'll never forget. She'd been a little star at the trial, a part of the jigsaw of truth that had helped to shatter Tracie's evil web of lies.

For Ray and me, it still seemed unbelievable that this was going to be just one of many family celebrations that we'd have to get through without Lee. Inevitably, with Tracie's appeal hanging over our heads, it seemed futile even to begin to try to pick up the pieces of our lives. And, because of everything Ray and I had said to the media about bringing back capital punishment for murder, we decided to start our own campaign calling for the Government to restore the punishment. It was something we'd always believed in, long before losing Lee, and, because Tracie's trial had attracted so much publicity, it made sense to capitalise on her conviction, and use her as an example in what we hoped might prove to be an equally high-profile media campaign.

Like all families of murder victims who are forced to deal with the anger and frustration of accepting the inevitability of an appeal against a life sentence for murder, we felt we couldn't just wait for the date of her hearing without channelling our energy into something positive. We wrote letters to everyone we hoped would not only be sympathetic but whom, we felt, might have some influence on bringing our campaign to fruition. The one to Tony Blair, reminding him that we'd talked briefly at the GMTV studios after the trial, made it clear that we were more determined than ever to make sure he knew we weren't alone.

Over time, we collected more than 10,000 signatures from people who supported renewed public debate on why the Government should consider capital punishment in dealing with convicted killers. We worked tirelessly on our campaign; our family, friends and neighbours all helped by getting signatures from colleagues and the E57 (a local social club that Ray has been a member of for 45 years) kindly provided headed paper for the petitions. We left no stone unturned when it came to gathering support: we stood outside the hair salon and asked the general public to sign; we trailed through pubs looking for signatures and we asked local businesses if we could leave the petitions in their shops and offices to be signed. Ray's work helped us out, as did West Midlands Travel, Lee's old employers.

We contacted the Home Office over the issue, and the response we had back from them in October 1997 was the first of many which made it clear that capital punishment is unlikely to ever be reintroduced in Britain. Parliament, we were told in no uncertain terms, had rejected its reintroduction by a substantial majority in 1994. The Government did not see it as a matter to be settled by a referendum as we were suggesting. A literal life sentence which results in an offender spending the rest of their days behind bars is only given when the gravity of the offence can only be reflected by a life term or if he or she continues to pose a serious public risk.

It was disappointing, but it didn't stop us going to London to hand in our petition and, to maximise publicity, Ray, Michelle and I turned up on the steps of Number 10 Downing Street on 1 December, the first anniversary of Lee's death. Our MP, Julie Kirkbride, whom we'd met while she was canvassing for the Conservatives in the run up to the 1 May General Election, came with us. We told the reporters who met us outside that we didn't want revenge; nothing could bring Lee back. We simply didn't want other parents to go through the agony of having to identify their child's body. We believed that the threat of a lethal injection was the only hard-line deterrent left open to a Government which seemed to be turning its back on the rise in violent crime. Never one to mince his words, Ray's answer to the problem was simple: 'Bring back hanging, and, if you can't find anyone to pull the rope, call me.'

Julie made the point that advances in DNA testing meant that it was a lot easier to prove someone was connected with a crime than it had been when the likes of James Hanratty and Ruth Ellis were making headlines. Like us, she still believes capital punishment is the only worthwhile deterrent for people like Tracie Andrews. She told reporters, 'No one can imagine Ray and Maureen's suffering over the last year as they have tried to come to terms with Lee's unnecessary death. They know the restoration of the death penalty can't do anything for Lee's case but it might help parents in the future when they have to come to terms with the murder of a child.'

Jack Straw, who was then Home Secretary, and Tory MP Ann Widdecombe met us and, again, gave us the prevailing view of Parliament. In *my* words, not theirs, pigs would fly and Lord Lucan would be found living in an old folks' home before anyone would see the return of capital punishment.

Far better, Jack Straw suggested, to campaign for life sentences to mean life, to make the Government realise that the only way to tackle violent crime was to ensure that those serving life sentences were never released.

It wasn't what we'd hoped to hear, but it made sense, especially as we still had no idea what Tracie's tariff would be. Anything we could do to make sure she stayed behind bars was worth considering and we said we'd return once our campaign was back on track.

That evening, we held a beautiful memorial service for Lee at St Nicholas's Church when friends and family gathered to celebrate his life at a service conducted by Eve Pitts. The image that will always remind me just how poignant it was appeared in our local morning newspaper, the *Birmingham Post*. It's a picture of Danielle and me. We're standing together in the church watching a candle flame. I have my arm around Danielle's shoulder. Her little face, so much like her dad's at that age, is filled with concentration as she holds the candle in front of her. It was hard to believe that a whole year had passed since Lee's death as we stood in the church with our family. Eve reminded us that Lee would have wanted it to be a happy occasion. It was, she said, a time of thanksgiving for his life.

I managed to hold back the tears as I read the passage Eve had helped me choose from Corinthians.

Ray was fantastic as he spoke about the pain of not being able to prevent Lee's death. He never faltered once as he read his tribute: 'In all the times in his life when he was in trouble or needed help, I wanted to be there for him,' he said. 'And yet the one time he needed me most, I wasn't there for him. He lost his life when I couldn't be there. It's only since Lee's death that I've realised just how special he was. He was a loving son and he loved his sister. Our loss is so enormous that only people who have lost children know how enormous it is. We're just so fortunate that he left his daughter Danielle, whom we treasure so much.'

After the service, we all went to the Bull's Head pub next door to the church with Brian and Mick and drank a toast to Lee. 'Let's try to move on and make the most of our lives together,' Ray said, slipping his arm around me. 'For Lee's sake and ours... Andrews may have destroyed his life but we can't let her destroy ours.'

I knew Ray was right. Our marriage had been stretched to its limits. And I knew he was as worried as I was that it might not survive if we didn't stop arguing and driving each other further apart. We were both drinking far too much, kidding ourselves that a bottle of brandy every night would help us dull the pain and block out reality. But, of course, it was only making things worse. The only time we didn't seem to argue was if we spent our evenings apart. Ray, slumped in front of the telly with a glass in his hand... me, crying in the bath or screaming and scrubbing myself red raw in the shower.

On Sundays when we weren't working, Ray would

disappear off to the golf club and I'd potter about the house on my own or go out somewhere with Danielle or Paige and Jordan. Like a lot of men, Ray had never been very good at dealing with his emotions. It wasn't that he didn't want to talk about Lee; he just couldn't. The only way he knew how to deal with his grief was to bury it, whereas I just wanted to get things out in the open. If it meant shouting and swearing, so much the better, regardless of whether or not I had someone to take out my anger on.

We'd both had enough of not seeing Lee. The pain of the physical separation was exhausting; it made us cry and shout. Sometimes alone, sometimes at each other. And, although Michelle and I were working hard, we seemed to be facing one staff problem after another. I'd have given anything to have closed the salon because I didn't have the heart or the energy to keep turning up.

But, because Ray had only just felt strong enough to go back to work, we badly needed the money. I couldn't just give it all up after Michelle and I had worked so hard to make it so successful. Looking back, it was only because I knew I had to keep going that I was unable to recognise how badly depressed I was. It was the same for Michelle. There were days when we could cope and others when we'd keep bursting into tears. One afternoon, as she was cutting a man's hair, she dissolved in tears and had to go into the back room. It broke my heart when she told me the man had had the same kind of hairline as Lee and, for a moment, she'd imagined she was cutting her brother's hair.

One girl who came in for a cut told her she hadn't had it styled since she'd left prison.

Michelle looked up from cutting her hair. 'Blimey,' she said. 'What were you in prison for?'

'I stabbed my boyfriend,' the girl said, casually flicking through a magazine. 'He was threatening to drop my baby over the balcony at our flat.'

Michelle had to wait until the girl had gone before she could disappear to the back room to have a good cry.

All of us wanted Lee to walk back through the front door and for things to be how they were. Sometimes, it helped to talk about how I felt to the clients, the ones I knew I could trust not to go running to the papers. But there were times when I was happier to listen to their problems rather than share my own.

I knew Ray was hurting like hell, especially after the way he and Lee had argued and had never had the chance to tell each other they were sorry. The guilt was gnawing away at him inside and, no matter what I said to persuade him that Lee wouldn't want to see his dad feeling that he alone was to blame, Ray didn't want to know. He'd never had the chance to make things right between them thanks to Tracie Andrews.

I didn't want to spend my days crying and looking at the photo albums. It was too painful. But, inevitably, on the days when I could hardly find the strength to crawl out of bed after another sleepless night, it was easier to wallow in grief rather than put on a brave face. Sometimes I'd even follow the number 35 bus, Lee's old route. I'd be driving along, see it going down the road in front of me and instinctively put my foot down on the accelerator to catch up with it. If I saw the bus going in the opposite direction,

I'd slam on the brakes and turn the car round. I'd imagine Lee was driving. In even crazier moments, I'd overtake and then look back to see if I could spot him smiling at me. It was madness. But no one knows how they're going to handle grief on such an enormous scale.

There are no textbook rules on how to behave. No words of comfort. You cling on to anything that you hope might block out the pain and reality of life without the person you've loved.

There was another reason, though, why Ray and I were falling apart. The night of Lee's death had been the last time he and I had made love. We'd gone to bed that evening after spending the day with my sister Josie and her two teenage children. It had been the first time we'd been to her home since her husband Simon had moved out, an occasion that had been tinged with the sadness of knowing our visit marked the beginning of their separation. It was a time to understand that, although Josie felt she had made the right decision to end her marriage, her children were clearly struggling with its finality.

In the car on the way home, I'd told Ray how it had made me appreciate our own marriage. I'd met Ray when I was 16 and, after 30 years together, our life with Lee and Michelle, despite the usual domestic ups and downs, was pretty much what we'd always hoped for. We were a middle-aged couple, easy in each other's company, thanking our lucky stars for what then had seemed such an ordered and secure relationship.

I often look back and wonder what our lives might have been like before the nightmare that began that night. We were living a life that neither of us could ever have imagined was about to be shattered forever.

For some inexplicable reason, what happened between Ray and me in the darkness that night was one of the most loving and memorable experiences we had ever shared as man and wife. Afterwards, as we'd been sleeping soundly in each other's arms, the police had arrived to tell us about Lee.

It was a sad, haunting and increasingly upsetting memory for me. Unlike Ray's guilt about his argument with Lee, my own was based on an appalling antithesis of pleasure and pain. Ray and I had been having sex while our son was being murdered. It wasn't an issue for Ray then or now. But it's one I'm still dealing with.

To say it put a spanner in the works in the year after Lee's death would be the understatement of the century. Intimacy of any kind between Ray and I, as far as I was concerned, was a complete no-no. Despite the dozens of occasions when we'd linked arms or held hands for the cameras during the trial, when we were alone, I'd flinch if he even accidentally brushed my arm. I felt terrible because he knew I couldn't handle the thought of being close to him. He was so kind, telling me he understood I needed time. But, because Ray couldn't reach out to meet me emotionally, the physical chasm between us got wider.

That night in the pub after Lee's memorial service, I knew it was down to me to try to put things right between us. You don't just stop loving someone after a lifetime together and I really believed our marriage was worth saving. If not for us, then for Michelle and Steve, Paige and

Jordan and Danielle. They'd already lost Lee; they didn't deserve to lose us. Mum and Dad... Nanny and Granddad.

Brian knew how I was feeling because he and I had often talked about how couples coped with the trauma of having a child murdered. The odds on our marriage surviving, he'd already warned me, were stacked against us but, if we were prepared to work at it, there was no reason why Ray and I couldn't be the two out of the eight couples that managed to hang on in there. 'You just need to be honest with each other,' he said. 'Think before you act and you'll get there in the end. Ray's a good bloke, Maureen. He loves you to bits. Anyone can see that. Mick and I see what's happening between you all the time with other couples who have gone through what you two are going through now. Only the strong survive. And I think you and Ray have definitely got what it takes to work things out.'

It was advice that came from the heart. It was down to me to carry on being strong for both of us.

Two days later, fate stepped in again. I thought Ray had been working late when the phone rang at 8.00pm on 4 December. His job as an HGV driver for Joseph Ash Galvanisers in Birmingham involved long hours but was helping him take his mind off what we were going through. I couldn't get my breath when a nurse at Sandwell Hospital explained that Ray had been involved in an accident at work.

'Oh, my God,' I yelled. 'Is he all right? What happened?'

The nurse said Ray was stable but had broken the fifth vertebrae in his neck. 'It happened this morning, Mrs Harvey,' she said. 'But he wouldn't let us contact you until he'd seen the consultant. He's going to be OK.'

OK? This woman had just told me my husband had a broken neck and, in the same breath, she was saying he was OK.

'What the hell are you doing to my family?' I shouted after I'd put down the phone and burst into floods of tears. It was question God hadn't been able to answer when Lee had died, so I wasn't surprised by the deafening silence in my head.

It was typical of Ray to try to protect his family from the horror of what had happened to him. I was so angry as I drove to the hospital but, by the time I arrived, I was beginning to understand why he'd insisted on no one telling me. He knew how hard I was trying to keep my head above water. He'd only felt mentally strong enough to return to work a couple of months earlier and, as money was so tight, I was working all hours at the salon to keep the wolf from the door. I'd taken so much time off for the trial that, despite the efforts of the staff to keep on top of the workload, I knew the business wouldn't survive without me back at the helm.

It was only when I got to the ward and spoke to Ray and his consultant that I realised how close I'd come to losing him. When he'd been brought into the hospital's A&E department that morning, no one had really believed he'd survive such a horrendous injury. The tears wouldn't stop as I gently held his hand and told him how much I loved him.

'I'm sorry, Maureen,' he whispered. 'I don't want to put you through this but, if I'm going to be paralysed, I don't want to be here.'

It was a stupid accident that could easily have been

avoided. Ray had gone to a trading estate in Tipton to pick up some steel girders but said he wasn't happy when he saw how they'd been loaded. It was a small yard so Ray climbed up to see if he could inspect them.

Again, typically thinking about others, Ray moved his lorry so that other drivers could get in. As he was trying to adjust the girders on his own, one fell off and hit him in the back of the head. Not realising he'd broken his neck, but feeling sick and giddy and with blood streaming from the back of his head, he'd staggered across the road to a garage. As soon as the two blokes working there saw the state he was in, they called an ambulance. Thank God – wherever the hell he was that day – one of them had done a first-aid course and told Ray not to move his head.

It had saved his life. The consultant told us that, if he'd put his head forward, the broken vertebrae in his neck could have severed his spinal cord. As if that wasn't enough, one of the male nurses at the hospital had recognised Ray from the papers. All he'd seemed bothered about as Ray was lying in bed, sedated in a neck brace with tears rolling down his face, was whether he was 'the bloke whose son had been murdered'.

Not knowing whether he'd walk again, Ray still hadn't lost his sense of humour. 'It's just as well for him that I can't bloody well move,' he told me. 'I'd have hit him so hard, he'd have needed more than a bloody neck brace.'

It was another devastating shock for us to deal with, made even worse by not knowing whether Ray's injuries would leave him in a wheelchair.

The tests seemed to go on for days as Ray remained

immobile in his hospital bed. Mercifully, he'd retained the feeling in his legs and arms but was terrified he wouldn't be able to walk or look after himself.

Michelle kept us going as she'd done in the weeks after Lee's death. There was no way her dad wasn't going to make a full recovery. Every day, she'd turn up at the hospital, smiling and cracking jokes to keep Ray's spirits up. When she cried, she always made sure it was never in front of us. Her optimism was our inspiration.

'We're going to get through this,' she'd tell me for the umpteenth time.

I felt ashamed that I couldn't share her determination. Seeing Ray, lying there in his hospital bed surrounded by monitors, not knowing what the future held for him was unbearable. I wanted to run away, to know that someone was going to be able to take care of me. I didn't want to be the one who had to keep propping up everyone around me.

Backwards and forwards I went to the hospital. Not eating and sick with worry that the salon would go under and take with it our only means of paying the bills, I barely survived. We'd already planned to cancel Christmas. At a time when families everywhere were looking forward to spending time together and checking their Christmas present lists, our lives had again been ripped apart. The decorations stayed in boxes in the attic and every card that came through the letterbox was ceremonially torn up after being opened and thrown away.

What had we got to celebrate? Ray stuck in hospital and the heartache of knowing that the only time Danielle saw her daddy was when she wiped his picture clean on his gravestone. She missed Lee so much. She missed him picking her up from school and helping her with her homework... gently tickling her back like he used to as she drifted off to sleep... taking her to the park. Tracie had stolen everything our precious little granddaughter had adored about her dad. It seemed so unfair.

I wanted Ray home but couldn't shake off the fear of not knowing how I'd look after him. There didn't seem to be anything certain in our future any more. We'd even had to cancel the holiday we'd been planning to take in January with Danielle to Disney World in Florida.

When he left hospital a month later, Ray's consultant assured us that, if he took it easy and kept up his weekly physiotherapy sessions, there was no reason why he couldn't make a full recovery. He'd been lucky but we all knew the hard work was only just beginning.

No matter how hard I tried to help Ray with his daily bed baths, dressing and feeding, I felt somehow that I wasn't making the grade. The depression that laid us both low in those first few weeks left us exhausted and volatile. And, just when I thought things couldn't get any worse, we found out that Lee's murder was being used to promote a film.

The Disappearing Act, starring Oscar-winning actress Patty Duke, had been released on video for the Christmas market. I wanted to be physically sick when I saw the cover. It showed a man's naked torso with a woman digging polished nails into his shoulders and the words 'SHE LOVED HIM TO DEATH – THE CHILLING STORY OF THE MURDEROUS INTENT BEHIND A FACE OF INNOCENCE'.

The blurb on the back of the DVD cover made reference

to the Tracie Andrews case, 'in which another glamorous blonde who pleaded innocence was convicted of the frenzied murder of her boyfriend.'

Local media had picked up on the story and the film's distributors admitted the text, referring to Tracie, had been specifically changed for the UK market. The idea that someone was trying to profit from our son's death was the last thing we'd expected, especially with his anniversary just around the corner. We told journalists it was sick and that the video should be removed from the shelves. Irene and Alan claimed they were considering taking legal action against the company.

In the 15-rated film, it was the parents of the 'glamorous blonde killer' who helped her dispose of her boyfriend's body – a twist that had left the Carters even more outraged than us. 'This video is outrageous,' Irene told the *Birmingham Evening Mail*, 'It makes no sense to say it parallels Tracie's case. Anyone who sees the film will get the idea we were involved in Lee Harvey's death. It's a nasty, cheap con – at our expense – to get people to rent a video.'

Irene said she'd referred the matter to Tim Robinson because she was concerned the film might harm Tracie's appeal. Unfortunately for her, it looked as though Mr Robinson had enough on his plate to be dealing with. If we needed something to smile about, we certainly found it when we read the closing paragraphs of the report.

That day, Tim Robinson and nine of his former legal executives were appearing in front of Stroud Magistrates, charged with conspiring to defraud the Legal Aid Board. 'What did I tell you?' said Ray, as he read me the details. 'It takes a crook to find a crook. It looks as though Robinson's going to find out what it's like to be on the other side of justice. I bet he'll need more than a hot bath and a bottle of plonk when he gets out of the dock.'

Mr Robinson did, indeed, look like he'd stepped up to his middle in brown sticky stuff. He was facing allegations of being involved in a plot to submit false claims for Legal Aid payment.

At the end of January 1998, Tracie, as we'd been expecting, was granted leave to appeal against her conviction. West Mercia Police told us they didn't know the grounds of her appeal but that it wouldn't be long before she'd be back in court.

Like me, Ray was trying hard to put on a brave face but I knew the frustration of not being able to work and needing my help to get around was getting him down. He was still in a lot of pain and, when I took off his neck brace to help him shave, I was terrified he'd move and aggravate his injury. A district nurse had shown me how to move his head carefully but I didn't have the patience, let alone the confidence, to do it. Especially when he moaned that I was hurting him.

I wanted to try harder and to prove that I could cope but we somehow reached the stage where we couldn't help each other. Ray, for all his faults, had at least been someone to turn to after Lee's death. He'd been strong enough to put up with my mood swings and angry tirades, but now he was understandably far more vulnerable than I'd ever seen him and I couldn't cope with treading on so many eggshells... eggshells that had already been badly damaged before his accident.

14

Edge of Reason

One morning, as I began Ray's nightmarish shaving routine, the tension between us exploded. 'For Christ's sake, why the hell can't you do this like the nurse?' Ray shouted.

I stood up, covered in shaving foam and threw his neck brace across the room.

'Fine,' I yelled angrily. 'Do it yourself. I've had enough of your moaning and whining. I know where I'm not wanted. I'm leaving you, Ray.'

The shock on Ray's face is something I'll never forget. He begged me to stay, hobbling across the room and wincing in pain, as he slowly bent down to pick up his neck brace. It was the cruellest thing I'd ever done but I just stood and watched him.

'I can't take care of myself right now,' I said, picking up my car keys and jacket. 'How the hell do you expect me to look after you?'

I don't know how long I spent driving round the roads near our home that morning. The tears were so bad, I could hardly see. But then I spotted the number 35 bus. I had to see Lee again. If I could just see his smiling face, things would be all right again.

I swung the car round into a side road, almost colliding with a van as I pulled out into a line of traffic. It was only when the familiar outline of the back of the single-decker was back in my sights again that I was able to slow down.

When people talk about having a nervous breakdown, it's hard to imagine what they really go through. What triggers a chain reaction of events in someone's life that takes them to the very edge of madness? We all deal with heartache, pain, grief and sorrow in different ways. We're lucky if we manage to keep a lid on our emotions and rationalise what we're going through. At the time, I was no longer able to control my emotions.

Driving along after that bloody bus, I was screaming, sobbing, banging the steering wheel. I didn't want to live like this any more, pretending that things were going to be the way they'd been when Lee was alive. Ray would be better off without me. The state I was in, I was only going to take him over the edge of the cliff with me.

Angry, sad and frustrated, I sat alone in my car until it was dark. I knew I should go back and tell Ray I was making the biggest mistake in my life, but I couldn't.

Michelle's voice was trembling when I rang her and told her I was leaving her dad. 'Mum, you're just upset. He'll understand how you feel,' she said. 'He needs you now more than ever... you can't leave.'

'I can't stay,' I sobbed. 'I can't get my head around any of this right now. I need some space. I'm having a nervous breakdown.'

I knew how much Michelle loved her dad and, looking back, it was that and the knowledge that she'd step in where I'd bowed out so shamefully that made it easier to go. I just felt that it was my turn to grieve for Lee. And I knew that, if I carried on trying to paint on a public smile while I was causing so much unhappiness and destruction in private with Ray, I'd end up going mad. I'd *gone* mad. There was no going back.

After staying with my sister Barbara for a few days, I knew I'd made the right decision. She'd seen what had been happening between Ray and me and she understood that I needed time to unravel all the negativity and anger that was pulling me down. Josie, my younger sister, was still going through the final stages of her divorce and said she had plenty of room to put me up. I could stay as long as I liked, she said. And, when the time came and I felt strong enough to pick up the pieces and fight, she'd still be there for me if I needed someone to rant and rave at.

Without her, I'd have been up the river without a paddle. It was such a relief to know that I was going to be able to make a new start. And, even if I was deluding myself, who else was there to blame but me?

I threw myself into working at the salon and even joined a gym. Michelle, to her credit, never tried to make me feel guilty but I knew how unhappy she was that Ray was having to cope alone. Typically, she just got on with things and, even though we were working together and there were plenty of opportunities for her to question my decision, she never judged me.

In those early days, after leaving Ray, I avoided asking her how he was doing. Every day she'd go round and see him, cooking, shopping and cleaning for him. She had Steve, Paige and Jordan to look after but it didn't stop her doing everything she could for her dad. I could walk out on him but she wasn't going anywhere. 'He's doing OK...' or 'He says hi...' or sometimes 'He's really missing you, Mum...' were the only bulletins I got. And, in my heart, I knew I didn't deserve to know anything. I was the one in the doghouse, the selfish bitch who'd thrown in the towel.

I was just grateful that Michelle hadn't turned her back on me. As the weeks passed, I got the feeling that she was not just making the best of a raw deal but that she understood why I'd left.

For Ray, things couldn't have got any worse. Physically helpless, out of work, alone and fighting severe depression, there didn't seem to be any reason why he would have wanted to carry on. It would be months later before he would admit to me that, during those dark days without Lee and me, he had contemplated suicide. Without Michelle's love and painstaking care, I don't think he would have been strong enough to cope. Death, as he told me, with the help of a bottle of brandy and some painkillers, would have been a welcome release.

Ploughing all my energy into the salon meant that it wasn't long before business was better than it had ever been. Ray and I had paid off our mortgage so I only had to help with his bills and managed to save enough for a deposit on a little house around the corner from Josie's.

But it didn't take me long to realise that living alone with barely enough money to cover my bills was far from fun. I had space and freedom to do what I wanted, but I was lonely. I felt a lot stronger both mentally and physically, but I wasn't happy. The guilt of knowing how badly I'd let my family down was always at the back of my mind.

In April 1998, the song 'Road Rage' by Welsh pop group Catatonia came into the charts. When I first heard it on the radio in the salon, I couldn't make out the words but had a horrible feeling that it must have something to do with Tracie. By the time I managed to get hold of a copy of it a couple of days after first hearing the song, the chorus was word-perfect in my mind. There had been enough clues to make me think that this was far from being a sick coincidence – 'home late', 'front page', 'outrage'... but, when I read the verse, I knew I had to give Warner's, the record company, a piece of my mind.

There was nothing I could do to get the bloody song banned but I wanted someone at the top to know how upset I was that people were dancing to a song all about Lee's death. And at least the group's lead singer Cerys Matthews had the decency to return my call and explain that she hadn't intended to cause any offence. She tried to convince me that the song showed how Tracie had gone crazy and that it didn't actually do her any favours. It was upsetting but at least I got my message across and, thankfully, none of the papers picked up on it.

With Tracie's appeal still hanging over our heads, I knew I didn't want to face the outcome of whatever decision the judges reached without Ray and Michelle by my side. It would have been easy to reach an uneasy truce with them and turn up as a family. But I didn't want to pretend we were united. Carrying on with my life apart from Ray was, in a way, acknowledging the damage Tracie had caused. If Ray would have me back, I had to try to make him believe that I was ready to try to make our marriage work.

Like all couples who have been together as long as we have, we had history. We'd had Lee. And, thank God, we still had Michelle and our precious grandchildren. I didn't regret walking out on my marriage but I knew I'd regret it if I didn't swallow my pride and ask Ray to forgive me. It wasn't easy for either of us to admit we'd lost sight of what was really important. Talking, shouting even, was part of being lost and not knowing how to cope with our grief. But listening to each other and accepting that there were bound to be times when we couldn't explain our feelings or face our fears would hopefully make a difference.

We both cried. Neither of us was perfect and losing Lee had, perhaps for the first time in our marriage, made us realise what a pair of stubborn old fools we were. Me and my big mouth, wading in for a fight before thinking about the consequences. Ray burying his head in the sand and hoping things would get better. We knew we had our work cut out and that it wouldn't be all hearts and flowers again overnight. But we were willing to give our marriage a second chance.

Two days before Lee's birthday on 20 September, a reporter from the *Sun* turned up with a video. The last thing we needed at a time when we were all feeling so sad and vulnerable was more questions about Tracie's appeal. But, when he told us that Tracie had sent the newspaper a video of a fashion show which had been held at Bullwood Hall Jail in Essex in which she had a starring role, we couldn't get him through the front door quick enough.

We couldn't believe it as we watched Tracie strutting down a catwalk amid cheers from the inmates in the audience. Dressed in tight black leather trousers, T-shirt and high heels, she was obviously having a whale of a time as she wiggled her backside and waved. The other prisoners were shouting, 'Tracie... come on, Tracie...' as she strode along the stage in time to the pumping dance music. With a ridiculous beret perched on top of her bleached-blonde hair, she was smiling and swinging her arms like some big butch dyke. And, judging by the size of her backside and saddle-bag thighs, it was obvious she'd been at the front of the queue in the prison canteen.

However sickening it was to watch, we needed to know that this was apparently how the murdering bitch was spending her life sentence. Not, as we'd hoped, locked up alone in a tiny cell, but enjoying the attention of a load of lesbian lags.

The reporter told us the show had been filmed by prison staff and Tracie had even styled inmates' hair for the occasion. There was even footage of Tracie hugging and kissing one of the organisers on the lips as she received a bouquet of flowers.

'It's great to know she's got a new girlfriend to help take her mind off Lee's birthday,' I told Ray.

We'd been in pieces on the day Lee would have been 27,

while Tracie had probably been cramming her fat arse into those God-awful trousers for a catwalk rehearsal.

Ray and I were more than happy to be quoted for the double-page spread that appeared in the paper the following day. If the world and its dog were going to see Tracie having such a good time, then we needed to remind everyone why she was serving life in the first place. The headline spoke for us: WHAT AN OUTRAGE – FURY AS ROAD-RAGE TRACIE HAS FUN AT JAIL FASHION SHOW.

And, just to make sure the Home Office knew how disgusted we were, I fired off an angry letter to Whitehall with a copy of the cutting. With just two weeks to go until Tracie's appeal, we just hoped the article would help damage her chances of it being successful.

The stress of not knowing what to expect was affecting my health far more that I wanted to admit to anyone. Some days I had to crawl on my hands and knees to climb the stairs because of the pain in my back. A cyst had started to grow on my spine and was pressing on my sciatic nerve. It was agony and meant I was on a short fuse for most of the time. Ray did his best to cope with my moody silences and kept reminding me that things would get better once the appeal was out of the way.

15

The Appeal

On 6 October 1998, the police took Ray, Michelle, Steve and me to the High Court in London for the hearing. Barbara and Josie had been so supportive that I wanted them to be there but Michelle wanted it to be just the four of us. It wasn't a case of her wanting to exclude them from anything; she told her dad that she simply didn't want it to turn into a travelling circus.

Ray and Michelle have always had a very special dad and daughter bond. She'd spent so much time looking after him when I walked out that it was only natural they would become even closer. And I think she felt he and I needed the time and space to heal all the anger and pain between us without the rest of our family being constantly involved.

We all knew our relatives were grieving just as we were and meant well, but, at times, it was suffocating and I could understand where Michelle was coming from. After Lee's death, it had got her down not being able to spend time alone with Ray and me because there always seemed to be someone turning up on the doorstep to make sure we were coping. After helplessly watching us fall apart and being there to pick up the pieces of our marriage, she was fiercely protective of us and wanted us to be able to move on with our lives without any well-intentioned interference.

But I still felt that Barbara and Josie had every right to come to the appeal. They'd been alongside us from day one and felt, as we did, that, even in the unlikely event that Tracie would be freed, we still had to stick together. Barbara and Josie sensed the tension when they turned up at court that day but, as they'd made the journey to London on the train, I didn't feel able to tell them not to bother coming back again.

It was interesting to see Tracie for the first time in more than a year as she came into the High Court dock flanked by two female prison officers. She saw us all sitting in the public gallery, but this time she defiantly held our gaze and even raised her head upwards a couple of times as if to show her contempt. The candyfloss blonde hair hadn't changed. Nor had the sombre black suit, demurely done-up white blouse or the trashy sling-backs.

But this time, there was an additional accessory – glasses. If they were meant to give her a sophisticated, intellectual appearance, then they didn't work. They made her look older, almost frumpy, serving only to accentuate the dark circles beneath her eyes and fatten her features. Did she really think that she was going home and that her conviction would be quashed?

Ronald Thwaites said the press coverage had resulted in Tracie not getting a fair trial. The media, he insisted, had portrayed her as 'an aggressive woman who devoured men, a female terrorist, a firebrand and a knife woman'. He admitted many of the stories had appeared as a result of her defence team's decision to ask for reporting restrictions to be lifted to encourage witnesses to come forward. 'The solicitor felt that the police had given up their search for the Sierra car too soon,' he said.

Although he said none of the stories had been in contempt of court, he said the trial judge Mr Justice Buckley had 'seriously underestimated' the risks of prejudicing potential jurors. 'Tracie Andrews' name and picture quickly became synonymous with unmitigated wickedness in the collective public mind,' he said. 'He failed to appreciate the enormity of prejudice that had been caused to this appellant by the publicity before the trial. He seriously underestimated the risks to a fair trial created by the pre-trial publicity, especially in the locality from which the jury panel was chosen.' Particularly damaging, he said, were the press reports alleging that Tracie had a history of violence towards former boyfriends.

Throughout the five-hour hearing, Tracie looked smug, triumphant almost, as she kept flicking back her hair and turning round to smile at her mum and dad. The only time she spoke was to confirm her name.

Our nerves were on edge as we listened to the case and watched the three judges making notes. The legal jargon used on both sides was, at times, beyond our understanding but we knew Thwaites wouldn't go down without a fight.

The police had warned us he'd try every trick in the book to get her out. Evil murderess or not, she was still his client. He even quoted a case which had gone before a judge years before, insisting that Tracie was just as much a victim as Lee and that her conviction was unsafe. The judge at her trial, he said, had failed to ensure the jury was not prejudiced and hadn't considered provocation and the alternative verdict of manslaughter rather than murder.

But Mr Crigman denied she'd had an unfair trial and that it had been Andrews and her lawyers who'd courted the publicity by going out of their way to maintain her innocence.

The judges, Lord Justice Roch, Mr Justice Laws and Mr Justice Butterfield, reserved their decision at the end of the day and adjourned the case for a week.

On 14 October, the decision we'd prayed for finally came. We didn't tell Barbara and Josie we wanted to go back to hear the decision without them. I wasn't happy about not giving them an explanation why and it caused a row between me and Ray and Michelle but I didn't want anything to upset Michelle. Lee was her brother; she'd been to hell and back and I could understand why she wanted it to be just the three of us. If things hadn't gone as we'd hoped and Tracie had walked, we wouldn't have been able to face anyone, not even our own family.

Tracie was still looking a bit too relaxed for comfort when we saw her again in the dock, and this time she'd gone to town on her outfit. As Mick commented during the adjournment while we having a coffee, 'Our Tracie's dressed to kill today.'

The mad staring eyes and bleached hair hadn't changed. But the skin-tight, white polo-neck jumper and figure-hugging black pencil skirt, split to the top of her thigh, proved she was obviously confident of the appeal going her way. The court was packed with reporters who were just as eager as we were to hear the judges' decision.

But, when we went back in to the court, after a brief adjournment, we knew there was something wrong. Tracie wasn't in the dock and the barristers and their legal teams were standing around talking to each other. When the judges finally came back in and announced their decision, I burst into tears.

Tracie had lost her appeal.

It was a significant ruling, not just for us but also, we felt, for the belief in the good sense of jurors.

Usually, when a defendant is charged with a crime, the media is banned from reporting more than the bare essentials of a case until it reaches trial. After Tracie was charged, it was her lawyers who'd chosen to lift reporting restrictions, thinking that it would improve her chances of being acquitted. The more publicity they thought they could generate, the greater the chance of her proving that a fat man with staring eyes had killed Lee. It was a tactic that we'd like to think backfired because it meant the case could be reported in far greater detail than would have been possible if reporting restrictions had been imposed. If Tracie's appeal had succeeded, it would have meant that reporting of criminal cases could have been circumscribed even further in future, and it would also have given other defendants the chance to follow the same course and use the same grounds for appeal. The ruling also implied that jurors can be trusted to put out of their minds anything they hear about a case outside the courtroom.

Before Tracie's appeal, the legal system had operated on the basis that jurors couldn't be trusted to use their common sense and reach a decision solely on what they'd heard in court. And yet, now, a Court of Appeal had upheld a conviction reached after widespread publicity about the case virtually from the moment Lee had been killed. By the time Tracie stood trial, it would have been difficult for any juror not to have known about the basic allegations. Yet they'd still managed to reach a verdict that no one except her thought should have been overturned. Maybe now, we thought, the law will credit jurors with more intelligence than in the past.

Outside the court, Steve Walters told us that Tracie had been given the news in the cell before the court had resumed. Her hysterical reaction didn't come as a surprise to us, nor did the fact that she'd had to be sedated. All that mattered was that she was on her way back to prison... where she belonged.

Michelle ordered two bottles of the best champagne as we celebrated with the police in a pub near the court that afternoon. I'd asked Brian to phone Barbara with the result of the appeal. I knew she and Josie would be upset that we hadn't told them the date of the appeal judgment, let alone try to explain why we'd wanted to go without them and I knew an inquisition would take the edge off the celebrations. He managed to tell her five minutes before it was announced on the television news which, understandably, went down like a lead balloon with her and the rest of the family.

Even when I later tried to explain my loyalty to Ray and Michelle, I could sense Barbara's disbelief and anger that I'd put my foot down and allowed them to have their way. The feeling of being torn apart is something that must be an occupational hazard in a situation like this. Of course, you need as much family support as you can get in the early days and aftermath of losing a loved one. And you have to recognise that relatives go through their own grieving process and need to feel they are doing their bit to help. You can't just open the front door and say, 'Right, we've drunk enough tea, everybody out, we need to be alone.' But, at the same time, if you don't find the courage to explain that you need space and time to preserve what's left of your sanity, inevitably the frustration turns to anger.

Barbara didn't speak to me for a while after the appeal and I don't think the close friendship we'd always shared as sisters has ever been the same. Neither of us is to blame. I've always been one to try to please everyone, so I'm sorry if anyone feels the barriers I put up at the time were intended to drive anyone away. They weren't. After losing Lee and then nearly losing Ray and our marriage, I had to hang on to him and Michelle.

The appeal was another milestone in our journey for justice but what we needed to know was what Tracie's prison tariff was likely to be. Knowing that her life sentence could never mean her spending the rest of her days behind bars, our only hope was that she would get the book thrown at her. Mr Crigman told us he thought she would serve a minimum of 14 years and that her tariff was unlikely to be set at anything more than 15. 'It's in the hands of the trial judge and the Home Office now,' he said. 'They're the ones who decide the minimum sentence to be served by someone who gets life for murder.'

It seemed incredible to us. Lee's life was worth more than 14 years. It didn't seem fair that she'd be released at the age of 42 and be able to restart her life with someone else. It made us realise that we couldn't just go home and try to get on with our lives without doing everything in our power to make sure Tracie served the highest tariff possible. Having got this far, we were determined to make sure our voice was heard. We would talk to as many journalists as possible and write as many letters to the Government as it took. Not just for Lee, but also for the families of other murder victims.

16

Tracie's Confession

In April 1999, we had a visit from a *News of the World* reporter. He had a letter he wanted us to have a look at. It was a copy of a letter Tracie had written in her cell in Bullwood Hall and had apparently planned to send to the Home Office via her legal team.

The reporter couldn't tell us how it had fallen into the hands of the newspaper or whether anyone was being paid for supplying it. But it was, he told us, something we'd definitely need to read sitting down.

Many of the reporters whom we'd spoken to after Tracie's trial had kept in touch with us. Knowing how keen we were to know what Tracie was getting up to inside jail, they'd ring us for a quote if they thought they had a story. We often joked about it when we picked up the phone and heard yet another journalist introducing himself. 'Hello, it's the Harvey rent-a-quote hotline here...' I'd feel like saying.

I'm sure not all families who find themselves on the receiving end of so much media attention in similar circumstances find it easy to deal with. The police offer as much or as little protection as you feel you need in the early days but, inevitably, if, like in Lee's case, they need the media's help in appealing for information and witnesses, you have to take a deep breath and get involved whether you want to or not. Until Lee died, the only experience we'd had of reporters and film crews was what we'd seen on the television or read about in the newspaper. You never ever think it's going to be you flinching in front of the flashlights or sobbing as you sift through boxes of family photos looking for ones of the child you're never going to see again. The phone never stops ringing, the letterbox keeps on banging and the envelopes containing interview requests pile up on your hallway table.

We're all different, and we all deal with the intrusion in our own way. You never lose sight of the fact that all reporters, no matter how sympathetic, how sensitive their approach, want a story. But, at the same time, there can be something deeply cathartic about talking to a stranger and taking control over what is being written about the person you've lost. For us, it was a mutual labour of love. After Lee's death, we wanted to catch his killer. After the trial, we wanted the world to know we'd never forgive Tracie. We wanted as much publicity as we could get for our 'Life for Life' campaign. And, when she was safely behind bars, we wanted to make sure we knew as much as we could about her prison life.

We knew she wouldn't fade into obscurity. We knew she

wouldn't go away. And it was purely because of that that we wanted to make sure she knew we weren't going to either. That's never changed – our breath will always be on the back of her neck.

Newspapers always pick up more stories about high-profile inmates than the police do because there are plenty of greedy prison officers and prisoners looking to make a few quid from passing on tips. We found that, by keeping in touch with the reporters who found out what Tracie was up to, they'd tell us before the story appeared in the papers. The ones who knocked on our door were nothing like the stereotypical images of hardened, chain-smoking, beer-swilling hacks we'd seen on the telly. If they did swill beer and chain smoke, they never did it front of us.

When the *News of the World* reporter turned up that day, Tracie had been keeping a pretty low profile after losing her appeal. So it came as a shock to discover she'd risked putting pen to paper, knowing her letter might end up making headlines. Was it salacious details of a fling with a lesbian lover? Another fashion show?

Ray and I were floored when we read the letter. Thank God, Lord Justice Roch, the appeal judge, had ruled there was nothing unsafe about her conviction. If he'd quashed her sentence and let her out, Tracie would never have resorted to this. She'd have literally got away with murder.

Here in black and white was Tracie's confession, proving, for the first time since Lee's death, that she was his killer. It had taken her two years and five months, but she was coming clean and finally admitting that she'd lied. Just as we'd thought, she'd concocted her road-rage story moments after repeatedly plunging a knife into Lee and callously watching him die.

The row between them at the Marlbrook pub, she'd said, had started because Lee was jealous of her relationship with Carla's dad Andy. The arguing continued in the car and, according to Tracie, both of them had said dreadful things, winding each other up about previous boyfriends and girlfriends. At one point, Tracie had got out of the car and, despite Lee's insistence that she get back in, she had refused. She stated that he had got out of the car and pulled a knife on her; a struggle had ensued during which she got hold of the knife and stabbed Lee in an effort to defend herself.

'I got back up and went to the car driver's side. I saw the case for the knife on the seat; I picked it up – and the black hat from down the side of the door. I threw down the hat and picked up the knife, put it in the case and put it down my trousers. I went over to Lee and knelt down, took off my coat and put it over him. I was then hugging him and crying, shaking and thinking, '"What have I done?"'

She claimed that it was at this point that she heard someone over at Keeper's Cottage so she screamed for help. As she and the man from the cottage were attending to Lee, the beam from the torch shone on the ground and she noticed a piece of the knife – so when he went back to the house she took the opportunity to put the piece of the knife in the case and back down her trousers.

She admitted that she had made up the story about her and Lee being attacked as she went along and she also stated that she had flushed the weapon down the toilet at the hospital.

On the subject of her suicide attempt, she said she had

wanted to try to kill herself before the press conference but that she had not had the opportunity. She had grabbed all the tablets that she could find in the house and swallowed them along with the ones she had been prescribed by the doctor.

'The more I keep things bottled up inside, the worse I'm making myself feel. I know that at the time I was ill. I was scared. I have been riddled with guilt over so many things. I made such a terrible mistake which I feel was forced upon me to do. I was in a no-win situation. I flipped and what happened next I will have to live with for the rest of my life. And so will Lee's family, my family, most of all my daughter and Lee's daughter. They have each lost a parent – even if they are in different contexts.'

It was hard for Ray and me to know what to think or say as we re-read the letter several times. Part fact, part fairytale, there wasn't a hint of remorse in her words, just a defiant insistence that Lee, not Tracie, was to blame for his death. As usual, she'd lied and twisted the truth.

The reporter wanted to know if we had any examples of Tracie's handwriting and her signature so he could compare it with what was on the typed letter. We had plenty. In the cards and notes we'd had from her over the years she'd been with Lee, her name had been scrawled on all of them. And, of course, it perfectly matched the one on her letter which she'd addressed from HMP Bullwood's C Wing with her prison number BE5110.

But, to us, this was no act of contrition. If she'd really wanted the Home Office to believe this was an admission of guilt, then why was she blaming Lee for her actions? Lee had never carried a knife. We'd always believed that Tracie had taken it out with her. He was no angel but there was no way he'd have pulled a knife on her. He'd always been the one to walk away from a fight, to try and calm Tracie down when she'd lost her temper and become violent. The knife wounds in his back proved that he was walking away, turning his back on her, when she stabbed him.

The reason why no one would ever believe that Lee had forced her to murder him was staring Tracie in the face, if only she'd been vaguely intelligent enough to realise it – he'd loved her. He'd loved her so much that he couldn't give her up. He couldn't drive away and leave her to walk alone down a dark country lane even when she was screaming and swearing at him.

She'd told lie upon lie after murdering Lee. She'd lied to the police, to the press, to the courts. Why should any of us believe she was telling the truth now? As far as we were concerned, the only thing we felt was true was the fact that she'd murdered Lee. Now Tracie had lost her appeal, there was no doubt in our minds that this was a meticulously planned and calculated attempt to save her skin. A key part of any inmate's rehabilitation lies in their ability to show remorse and admit their crime. Saying 'sorry' gets you back on the road to Home Office redemption; it gets you privileges, parole.

Our phone didn't stop ringing the next day when the headline TRACIE ANDREWS' SHOCK CONFESSION – I WAS ROAD RAGE KILLER was splashed across the front page of the paper next to a photo of Tracie. Inside, beneath the headline WORLD EXCLUSIVE – ROAD-RAGE BLONDE REVEALS HOW SHE BUTCHERED HER LOVER, was a full transcript of her letter.

The next day, when we saw the *Daily Mirror*, Tracie's revelations appeared to have come as just as big a shock to her mum. 'I'm bitterly angry and very upset,' Irene had told the paper. 'The first I knew was when I read the paper. She has never given me an inkling.'

But for the first time, just as Ray, Michelle and I had always suspected, Irene had also admitted that she had thought Tracie was guilty. It wasn't something she'd ever chosen to share with the police or us.

'Right from the start, there were some things about her story which just didn't add up,' Irene said in the article. 'Before Tracie was arrested, she was living with us and I asked her stepfather to get her drunk one night to try and get at the truth. They saw off a bottle of vodka between them, as well as wine, but still Tracie didn't make a slip.'

That week, I wrote a letter to Tracie. She could ignore the comments Ray and I had made in the paper about her confession but there'd be no escaping a sealed envelope sent to her at the prison. I addressed it to Tracie Andrews – Murderess – Lifer.

The day my son Lee brought you home to my house he was so happy and proud to show you off. For his sake, I tried to like you and see the nice side of you like he did. But I didn't like you from the start. I could see you had loads of problems, hang-ups and a serious problem with jealousy. You are self-centred and always had to have your own way. You were moody and just loved yourself.

My family and I tried for Lee's sake to make you

welcome but knew in our hearts that you were a liar and a cheat. You spoiled most of our family get-togethers with your moods and we had to put up with them time and time again because of Lee.

You lied, Tracie Andrews, about losing Lee's baby. You said it was a miscarriage and you fell down some steps in Redditch. Lies again!

Lee and the rest of my family felt sorry for you. We were very upset – especially Lee – we came to see you. We were sad. You took your baby's life and then you murdered its father, my son.

Michelle and Ray knew right from the start that you'd murdered Lee but I wanted to believe your story. I wanted the truth to come out and gave you the benefit of the doubt for Lee's memory. Because I knew my son loved you. But as the days went on and your story started to break up, the evidence became overwhelming... I realised what a scheming, lying bitch you are. You lied so much that you could not go back. And now, you have all the time in the world.

You've probably been told by your family of inmates that the only way you'll get an early release is to confess. But you've even had to lie about that and twist the truth. Lee's not here to give his account of that night and you lied. You're lying now.

One day, they just might let you out and I want to tell you how much I'm looking forward to that day. I'll be waiting for you. I have a lot of time, too. But I won't be as nice as the last time when I held your murdering hand. And you have to answer to God. Do you know what you have to answer for? Do you realise what you have done?

You stabbed Lee. The man you loved and who loved you more than life itself. You stabbed him 42 times – I know, I had to identify him. I saw what you did to him. You are a cold-blooded killer. You robbed Ray and I of our son. You robbed Lee of his life. You robbed Danielle of a dad. She is really in a bad way... she misses him and hates you so much.

You robbed Michelle of a brother – she hates you, too. Words cannot say how you have wrecked her life. You have destroyed our family. We hate you and wish that Lee had never set eyes on you. You mad, fucking bitch. I wish you were dead.

I feel sorry for your daughter, having a mum from hell. She must be so ashamed of you. You can never find a nice person inside you because there isn't one there.

You can't turn back the clock. There are no second chances. You will never find peace because you committed cold-blooded, premeditated murder. And the world knows it. You deserve everything you get.

You would have done all of us – Carla, your family and ours, and yourself – a favour if you'd made a better job of your suicide attempt. Better luck next time, bitch.

We hear you're a lesbian now. Sleep well. We'll see you when you get out. Sweet dreams.

Maureen

I have never regretted writing and sending that letter to Tracie. I'm sure she's always known how I feel but we were all so angry that she didn't have the courage to confess to killing Lee after she'd done it that I had to let her know. The contempt we felt at knowing she'd waited until her appeal had failed before admitting her guilt is as raw now as it was then.

Dealing with the anger we all felt about the way Tracie had admitted what she'd done was, I think, almost as difficult as coping with the grief. It somehow seemed worse because I'd so badly wanted to believe her road-rage story and had gone along with her cruel charade during the police press conference. The sense of betrayal was overwhelming and I wasted a lot of time trying to figure out in my own head why I hadn't followed the same instincts as Ray and Michelle.

Why, when she knew how much I'd loved my boy, could she not have told me the truth and said she was sorry? Of course, it wouldn't have brought Lee back but it was the only thing she could have given me after turning our world upside-down.

Anger is such a deeply destructive emotion and dealing with it when you're grieving at the same time feels like a kind of madness. I didn't want to be angry with anyone. I wanted to try and pretend that I was getting on with my life and that what Tracie had done to us wasn't affecting our lives. But it was. And always will.

One of the saddest consequences of this was losing my business. I'd owned six hair salons before 1995 and their success was due entirely to all the hard work that Michelle and I put into running them. Our clients were loyal, our staff was dedicated and business was going from strength to strength. But taking so much time off during the trial and after Ray's accident had a big impact on customers booking appointments. We were taking more money out to cover our bills than was going in.

The time I spent building it back up with Michelle after I'd left Ray probably saved me from a nervous breakdown but the financial rewards just didn't seem to matter as much. Hardly a week went by when someone didn't come in and start talking about the trial or what they'd heard Tracie was supposed to be doing in prison. They would want to know how we were feeling, how Danielle was coping without her daddy, the sort of questions we couldn't even answer within our own family, let alone share with strangers.

In September, a few days after what would have been Lee's 27th birthday, I just decided I'd had enough of pretending that I was coping with running the business. It happened shortly after I turned up for work one morning. I was standing alone in the salon wondering what on earth the point of it all was and just started smashing everything off the shelves. If someone had looked through the window or opened the door, they'd have probably had me arrested.

I collapsed on to my knees in tears on the floor and decided it was time to move on. Whatever it took to pay our bills, Ray and I would just have to survive.

17

The Tariff

On 3 November 1999, we received a letter from the Prison Service telling us that the Home Office had set Tracie's sentence tariff. In line with recommendations of the trial judge and the Lord Chief Justice, it was 14 years – the minimum period required to be served for what the letter described as 'the purposes of retribution and deterrence in respect of the offence'. She wouldn't be automatically released once the 14 years were up but only after a favourable risk assessment by the Parole Board.

As we'd been told by the police, the Home Secretary would decide when she'd be freed after considering whether she was safe to release and the public acceptability of her leaving prison.

We'd wanted life to mean life. There was no comfort in knowing that she'd come out on a lifer's licence and could be recalled for bad behaviour. And it didn't help to know that 'any concerns expressed by the victim's family' would be taken into account and included in her life licence when her release was being considered.

Surely, Lee's life was worth more than 14 years. Tracie's release, if it really was a possibility after serving her minimum tariff, would enable her to start her life again at the relatively young age of 42. It's a number I'm never going to forget because she stabbed Lee 42 times.

We felt the punishment should fit the crime. There was no way that 14 years could ever reflect the life, the future, that Lee could and should have had.

A month later, among the letters we received in response to the angry ones about Tracie's tariff we had fired off to our list of Home Office contacts, was one from Ann Widdecombe. Julie Kirkbride had told her we were hoping to revisit her and Jack Straw to find out if there was anything we could do to get it increased.

Naturally, Ann said she was sorry for our suffering and hopeful we'd be able to move on with our lives, but she didn't think life *should* mean life. The mandatory life sentence, she said, was introduced as a substitute for the death penalty. But, just as the death penalty only applied to a smallish number of murders, so the same, she felt, was true of the whole-life sentence, which is largely given for acts of terrorism and premeditated murder involving multiple victims.

'Below whole life, the tariff is set at different levels to reflect the degrees of culpability,' she wrote. 'I'm sure we would all acknowledge that someone who kills in, say, a drunken rage, is culpable, but not as culpable as someone who plans and conspires to kill several children. There must, therefore, be a range of tariffs.'

On the eve of Lee's third anniversary in December 1999, there were more media reports about Tracie. This time the reports concerned an independent television company planning to interview her in her prison cell.

We just couldn't understand why the media were so interested in Tracie's prison life. There seemed to be convictions for murder or trials opening and closing every time we turned on the television news. What was so fascinating about a dysfunctional, psychotic liar who had shown no remorse for her crime? Why this apparently insatiable need to sensationalise Lee's death in some cheap documentary about women who murder?

To us, Tracie Andrews always was and always will be a nobody. It was horrendous to think she was going to get the opportunity to talk about what she'd done, not just to Lee but to us. Her life sentence had stripped her of all human rights and privileges; she didn't deserve a starring role in a programme to justify her actions.

According to the reports about the television company's plans for the three-part series, entitled *Trail of Guilt*, Tracie was keen to tell the truth. It was sickening. She'd had five weeks to tell the truth in court and, instead, she'd come up with a pack of lies. The idea that the company would focus on the role of forensic scientists within a murder investigation was just an excuse to wheel Tracie out in front of a camera.

We contacted Julie Kirkbride and asked her if she could set up another meeting with Jack Straw to ask if he could make sure Tracie was denied another five minutes of fame. It was such a relief when we saw the letter he'd written to her:

> *The Prison Service has received a request to interview Tracie Andrews and another life prisoner for a documentary on women who murder.*
>
> *The requests will be declined in line with the Service's policy of not allowing interviews with individual prisoners except in cases where a miscarriage of justice is alleged.*
>
> *The protection of victims and their families from further pain is of paramount importance to the Prison Service when considering such requests.*

Typically for us, the grey cloud that accompanies every silver lining returned within a few days in the form of an opinion piece by the *Birmingham Evening Mail*'s columnist Maureen Messent.

In her view, the bereaved parents of a murdered child focused on the killer with growing hatred because, unlike accidental deaths, murder is avoidable.

Ray and I, she suggested, were inflicting pain on ourselves by saying Tracie's 14-year tariff wasn't long enough and would be better off letting our vengeance go instead of nurturing it.

'Surely it is wiser for them not to shout that 14 years isn't long enough,' she'd written. 'The law is not for punishment alone. Prison sentences are to rehabilitate as well. Andrews, whose crime shocked us, won't be more rehabilitated by serving longer.

'In France, remember, she would have been likely to walk free on the grounds of her killing being a crime of passion. And like Lee, she too has a child. Above all else, her real punishment will be her knowledge that she took the life of the man she apparently loved. Remorse, say the psychiatrists and grief counsellors, can be a heavier burden at times than loss.'

Everyone knows that columnists invariably play devil's advocate when they choose an opinion topic. Controversial commentary provokes the reader and invites allegiance or adversarial reaction. But, when it's personal, when it's *your* loss, *your* grief, you can't help but feel defensive, hurt and angry.

The letter I wrote in response was from the heart and printed in full.

> *What gives you the right to tell us how we should feel, whether it is hatred or any other emotion you care to name regarding Lee's murder, when you are so clearly not qualified to do so? You have no children so you can have no idea how we feel. In fact, in your wildest dreams, you cannot imagine how we feel both individually and as a family.*
>
> *Even people with children have no idea, although they are better qualified than you to begin to understand the pain we live through every day of our lives. We are serving a life sentence.*
>
> *You refer to what happened between them seconds before she murdered Lee. Only one person knows the answer to that but, whatever took place, that did not*

give her the right to brutally murder our son. And have you asked yourself what she was doing carrying a knife unless she intended to use it?

You also mention remorse. She has never shown any because she is a convicted killer, who, through lying, thought she could get away with murder. She lied for over a year, costing the taxpayer a fortune. She only confessed after a failed appeal which left her with no way of lying her way out. She confessed when she was told it was her way of getting parole.

As for the 14 years, we are not inflicting pain on ourselves or twisting the knife. We don't have to. She has already done that "over 40 times". She took Lee's life and she should spend the rest of her natural life in jail. Life should mean life.

If you were ever unlucky enough to have a member of your family murdered, we are sure that you would write a different article. It's getting close to Christmas. Lee's daughter Danielle, who has suffered the greatest loss of all, will open her presents on Christmas morning with the knowledge that she will never feel her father's arms around her, or hear the words he always said to her... "Love you."

When Lee's sister, Michelle, lays the table for Christmas dinner for the family, there will always be an empty chair.

Think of these things, Maureen, before you intrude into things you know nothing about.

We met Jack Straw again on 17 February 2000. It was a 45-minute meeting and we didn't pull any punches. If Tracie's tariff couldn't be increased, then we wanted an assurance that she'd be banned from returning to Birmingham after her release. We told him that, if we ever came face to face with her, we couldn't be responsible for our actions.

He told us that ministers wanted the rights of victims and their families to be given priority over those of criminals and assured us that a condition of Tracie's licence would be living outside the city. European laws meant that she couldn't be kept inside for life but she would still have to serve her tariff before being eligible for parole.

Even though it seemed like we'd reached the end of the line as far as hoping for a government review of life sentences, the meeting still felt like a victory of sorts. To have had the sympathetic ear of the man who oversaw Home Office policy made us feel that, even if we couldn't expect radical changes in the sentencing laws, we still had a voice. And at least Tracie wasn't going to be allowed to be interviewed on the television.

There was more to celebrate that month when the company behind the documentary announced it had abandoned its plans.

If only it had ended there.

18

Facing the Future

In May 2001, Ray and I decided that we wanted to do something special to help us get back on track with our marriage. It hadn't been easy for us to pick up the pieces when I came home after leaving Ray, but sharing the same house, if not always the same bed, was the best starting point we could hope for.

Inevitably, there were days when the only way of coping with the grief was to just take off on our own and have a good cry where no one could see us. One of the most comforting things for me was visiting Lee's grave. I could sit alone talking to him for hours or just spend the time thinking about happier times we'd spent together as a family.

For Ray, it was watching a game of football on the telly or, on the days when the constant pain from his neck injury was bearable, a round of golf with one of his mates.

We kept in touch with the Reverend Eve Pitts because she was so supportive and kind and we felt that she was one of the few people in our isolated little world who genuinely didn't mind when we called her for a chat. She was delighted when we told her how determined we were to save our marriage.

'What you need is something to help you mark this new beginning of yours,' she told us. 'You've had your share of unhappiness... you need to put it behind you and get closer to each other and God.'

And that was how Ray and I ended up renewing our wedding vows with Eve, our divine inspiration, alongside us at the altar. It was a wonderful occasion. Danielle and Paige looked like princesses dressed in gold tiaras and beautiful ivory gowns with tiny rosebud straps. Jordan, with his hair cut to perfection in the latest style, wore a black suit with an ivory-and-gold waistcoat. His uncle Lee would have been so proud of him. He looked so handsome and stole the show.

Ray wore a black dinner suit and I looked the part in a long gold halter-neck silk dress with a matching bag and shoes.

It was a wonderful service and, as Ray and I knelt at the altar, Eve told the congregation she had left a space next to us for Lee. You could have heard a pin drop when she said that. We felt so close to Lee and filled with peace, although it was emotional to listen to Eve talking about how Ray and I had managed to survive too many dark moments to throw away what we had between us. She talked about how strong Michelle and Steve had been for us, how Paige and Jordan had kept us going and how Danielle would always be a shining light in our lives, just as she'd always been for her dad. Eve made the day so special, making the congregation cry as she reminded them of so many memories of Lee and then making us all laugh with her jokes.

As Ray and I walked back down the aisle in front of our family and friends, the sound of the song 'Endless Love' filled the church. It has always been a special song for Ray and me and we could still hear the words as we stood in the church doorway being showered with confetti.

Eve and her husband Anthony joined us afterwards at the party we held at the E57 social club where both Michelle and Steve, as well as Lee and Tracie, had celebrated their engagements. Ray even took me there on our first date together when I was a shy 16-year-old. It was a little pocket of happiness, a reminder that, even if our lives had changed and nothing would ever be able to help us get over losing Lee, then at least we had each other.

They say you can't teach an old dog new tricks, but I think that knowing how close we came to splitting up made Ray and I appreciate what we had together. It's not perfect. I'm not saying it ever will be, but marriages that run the course and survive are well worth hanging on to.

I lost count of the number of times I wrote to the Home Office that year complaining of stories about Tracie which seemed to keep turning up endlessly in the papers. First, there were rumours, quickly scotched by the Home Office, that Tracie was planning to write a book. Then she'd apparently re-enacted the shower stabbing scene from the Alfred Hitchcock thriller *Psycho* in front of inmates at Bullwood Hall. Next came the sensational *News of the World* headline HAIR RAISING – ROAD-RAGE FIEND LEARNS HOW TO TRIM LOCKS IN PRISON.

And, a month later, another story in the *Sun* appeared, headlined: THE ANDREWS SISTERS – MURDER GIRLS WHO SHARE THE SAME NAME MEET IN PRISON AND BECOME BEST PALS.

The first one beggared belief. Six months after starting a hairdressing course in Bullwood Hall, Tracie was happily charging inmates and prison officers a pound a time for cutting their hair. One officer had even been quoted as saying how brave her customers had to be knowing her history with a pair of scissors in her hand.

My letter of complaint had only just gone off to the prison Governor when we saw the news that Tracie had befriended convicted killer Jane Andrews. The *Sun*'s story said that Jane, who'd worked for Sarah Ferguson, the former Duchess of York, as her dresser for nine years before being jailed for life for the murder of her boyfriend, had met Tracie in Bullwood Hall's lifers' section. An inmate had told the paper, 'Jane has found Tracie very supportive. She is one of the Queen Bees of the prison with a very outgoing personality. All the inmates are very curious about Jane because of her royal connections. But, with Tracie as her protective friend, she knows she won't be bothered by the other girls.'

Warders had even nicknamed them 'The Andrews Sisters' after the US wartime trio who became a favourite with troops. It was easy to see what Tracie and her new best friend would have in common. Jane Andrews had been given a life sentence in May that year for savagely attacking Tom Cresswell with a cricket bat because he refused to

214

marry her. They'd have so much to talk about over a cup of prison tea. Maybe even swapping tips on the best way of making troublesome boyfriends bleed to death or how to get the best price for a slightly used engagement ring.

We were outraged. Did we really deserve to know that Tracie was apparently having a far more interesting life behind prison bars than when she'd pulled pints behind the bar of her local? The idea that she was being allowed to have any kind of power or status really riled me. She seemed to be having an easy time while we were the ones doing the life sentence on the outside.

When the Prison Service didn't return my calls asking for Tracie to be moved to a tougher prison so she could experience a far stricter regime, I sat down and wrote a letter. I stopped short of suggesting that the Governor might even like to consider giving me a job teaching hairdressing to the inmates. Tracie wouldn't be quite as cocky if she saw me striding down the lifers' wing with a pair of scissors in my hands. I wrote:

> *We are absolutely outraged that Tracie Andrews is allowed to run your prison. She is obviously 'Top Dog' or 'Queen Bee'. And a member of your staff appears to be making a mockery of the Prison Service by selling stories about her to the newspaper. She has been sent to prison to be punished for murdering our son and, instead, she seems to be living in a holiday camp.*
>
> *Do you think that a cold-blooded murderer should be allowed to use a pair of scissors to cut people's hair after what she's done? Especially when bits of*

215

*scissors found at the crime scene pointed to the fact
that she used the scissor part of a knife to stab our
son over 40 times. I think a lot of people would find
this completely unacceptable.*

*We want Tracie moved to another prison where she
might not be quite as comfortable and are going to do
everything in our power to get it done. You are the
prison Governor and the one who is supposed to run
the place, not her or anyone else.*

*To be frank, we don't think you or your staff are
doing a very good job. We know that inmates are
supposed to be rehabilitated but they should not be
allowed to take part in fashion shows or prance
around with dangerous weapons acting out scenes
from Psycho. This is not acceptable.*

Maureen Harvey.

The response I received from Beverley Hughes, the then
Parliamentary Under-Secretary of State, said that Tracie
had given her consent to release information about herself:

*Ms Andrews is currently studying for her NVQ Level 3
in advanced hairdressing and studies and works in the
hairdressing salon. It is only since she has embarked
on her Level 3 NVQ that she has done any cutting of
hair and, according to the hairdressing instructor, she
has cut hair only on a dozen occasions. On each of
these occasions, she has been fully supervised by her
instructor. She does not receive payment for this work.*

As to the appropriateness of this situation, one of the objects of the Prison Service is to reduce crime by providing constructive regimes which address offending behaviour, improve educational and work skills and promote law-abiding behaviour in custody and after release. The facilities and opportunities Ms Andrews has availed herself of whilst in custody are entirely in keeping with this objective. The benefits of such an objective are clear when one considers Ms Andrews's good conduct and progress thus far in her sentence plan.

She would be periodically risk-assessed during her sentence. Furthermore, when a prisoner applies for employment or access to educational facilities within an establishment, their suitability is rigorously assessed before they are allowed to partake. This, combined with the fact that she was supervised at all times, ensured that any potential security risks would have been negligible.

I am of the view that allowing prisoners to study and work to acquire work skills and earn qualifications plays a key role in assisting them to address their offending behaviour and equips and prepares them for their eventual return to the community. As such, it is entirely appropriate that, with due regard to any security implications, prisoners are encouraged to work and study to this end.

I am able to confirm that Jane Andrews and Tracie Andrews spent a few days working in the prison shop where Tracie helped to train Jane. They both reside on the Lifer Wing. There is no suggestion of any relationship between them. In claiming that they have "teamed up", the media is overstating the matter.

The establishment does not feel it is appropriate or fair to consider transferring Ms Andrews at this stage and refute any suggestion that she "has things well organised for herself".

While I sympathise fully with the victim's family, no useful purpose would be served by transferring Ms Andrews who has made good progress whilst at Bullwood Hall Prison.

So now we know, I thought. Just so long as Tracie is getting on with her rehabilitation, maybe even advancing her educational plans at the taxpayers' expense to become a barrister or a brain surgeon, we can get on with our lives and wait for the next newspaper article. If the inmates convicted of poisoning their victims aren't too busy preparing the meals in the prison canteen, maybe they'd like to have a go at cutting hair in the salon as well. And the arsonists... why not let them stage a firework display on Bonfire Night?

It was at times like this that I felt like running away. We all did. Every time something appeared in the papers, we were besieged by reporters, well-wishers who wanted to let us know they, too, were outraged and phone calls from friends and relatives wanting to know how we felt. We felt angry. Bloody angry. But there was nothing we could do about it.

Four months later and, bingo, there was yet another story in the *Sun*. This time the headline was KISS OF LIFER – KILLER ANDREWS SAVES DYING WOMAN IN JAIL.

This story really took some believing. Tracie had apparently been awarded an official commendation for 'meritorious conduct' after giving the kiss of life to an inmate at Bullwood Hall. Even more astonishing to us was the suggestion that her actions could earn her an early release.

The incident involved a 24-year-old woman named Lisa Davies who had been given a life sentence for grievous bodily harm two years earlier. Tracie had apparently found her collapsed outside her cell with tape around her face, nose and neck in what was described as a cry for help that had gone too far.

I got straight on the phone to the Governor, Tony Hassall, demanding to know whether it was true and why we were being subjected to such distressing stories in the papers. He was full of apologies, but said it was virtually impossible to stop or reduce stories being leaked to the press especially when an inmate was as high profile as Tracie was. But he knew nothing about her being involved in an incident where she'd saved someone's life. The only assurance he could give me was that no one was being considered for early release and said he would investigate and let me know the outcome. He said there had been a self-harm incident within the prison which had been dealt with by officers but had not involved Tracie.

Needless to say, I fired off yet another letter to the Home Office to make sure they knew how upset and angry we were, and I wondered how much more of this gradual drip-drip-drip of stories about Tracie we would have to endure.

19

Among Friends

One of the most enduring, inspirational lifelines we had as a family in the darker days immediately after Lee's death was our contact with the Victims of Crime Trust. Its founder, Norman Brennan, is a former policeman who decided to set up the charity in 1994 to help people like us cope with their loss.

Until Lee's death, we'd never heard of the organisation and, when Norman phoned me after reading about Lee in the papers, our first thought was that it wasn't something we needed. But, after a while, we thought it could be a way of getting some help and, even at that stage, we felt we wanted to help others like us.

Like so many families in our shoes, we hadn't been offered any formal counselling and, when Norman said he could put us in touch with other victims' families if we ever felt we'd like to share what we were going through, it was like someone switching on a light. It's a club that no one ever chooses to join because no one ever thinks what happened to families like ours is ever, in a million years, going to happen to them. But, if it does, then it's deeply comforting to know you're entitled to automatic membership.

Norman explained that, having compared the support networks offered to victims and offenders, he'd realised there was an urgent need to offer emotional and practical help to families who were simply left alone to pick up the pieces of their lives. Offenders get help from all sides from day one; people on hand to explain their legal rights, medical assistance, rehabilitation in prison... basically, anything they need to help them through the criminal process. Victims are lucky if they get a cup of tea and a plastic carrier bag full of bloodstained clothing.

Shamefully, there are more than 100 support groups for criminals but only one, the Victims of Crime Trust, offering professional back-up for the families who have lost a loved one at the hands of a killer.

Norman was a good friend to us and possibly one of only a handful of people whom we felt we could relate to when our world was falling apart. Clive Elliott, who gave up his job as the manager of a satellite TV company to help Norman run the charity, is one in the same mould.

Considering that one in three bereaved relatives contemplate suicide within three months of losing a loved one, the task of trying to help them face the isolation of grief and the practicalities of the police investigation and court process is far from enviable. We had friends and relatives who didn't know what to say to us or do. It's no one's fault. It's just that no one would choose to spend more time than they feel they have to with people like us. If you haven't been through it, it's impossible to understand the effort it takes to even get out of bed some days, let alone worry about what's in the fridge or when the ironing's going to get done. You don't plan, you just do the best you can to survive.

One of the most inspirational things about the charity is being able to talk to other parents and relatives whose loved ones have died years before. Knowing that these people were still surviving years later gave us the strength to carry on at the time. Like them, all we could do was get through one day, another night, and then another day. Some days we'd feel really strong and felt ready for anything life could throw at us, but there were others when we'd collapse crying and screaming, not wanting to face the world.

By speaking to others who didn't have to pretend they understood how we felt, we got through so many dark days and nights, sharing our fears about a future without Lee, and gradually feeling stronger and believing that we would eventually feel able to plan and hope.

Norman was passionate about helping victims' families and told us he would always only be a phone call away if we ever needed him. We often phone him for advice all these years later.

Ray, Michelle and I raised loads of money for the charity; looking back, it helped to be able to channel some energy into such a good cause. And listening to other bereaved parents – many of whom endured the nightmare of inconclusive murder investigations with their children's bodies or killers still remaining undiscovered – was a salutary distraction from my own moaning, making endless cups of tea and grieving alone.

Many other victims phoned me for advice. One lady, when she realised we were ex-directory, phoned every Harvey in the book until she found Ray's nephew, who then passed her number on to us. Her name was Jane Smith and her brother had been stabbed several years before Lee in a pub after a row over a girl. The killer never admitted the crime and spent years in prison trying to clear his name. Her family hadn't received any counselling or advice and she said she was impressed that we were fighting for such a good cause. We met up and became friends and I told her how to get information about discovering her brother's killer's tariff, getting information from the Government and helping her to contact her MP. Just like us, joining the charity gave her a voice and, when her mum died soon afterwards, it must have been very comforting for her to know that she wasn't alone.

Another lady stopped me in the street, having seen me on the television, and told me how brave she thought I was. Her son Stephen had been murdered after being stabbed and hit over the head with a car jack while trying to help a girl who was having a row with a taxi driver. She and I were best buddies within ten minutes of meeting and we went out together regularly. Her marriage had broken up because of what had happened and she told me she was going through so much grief that she couldn't even face visiting her son's grave.

I told her that we all cope differently and deal with the

grief in different ways. That there were no rules, no pills, no prayers, no magic wands; you just had to do whatever you could and gradually find your own way back.

Stephen was in the same cemetery as Lee so, eventually, we started going together. She found it hard but felt better for going. I often visit his grave when I go to see Lee's.

Just as I was there for her when she needed me, she was there for me when I left Ray. We'd go out for a drink together and I'd do her hair for her to cheer her up. We still see each other. Both of us know that, even though the grief never goes away, you just learn to live with it.

Having received so much kindness from Norman and Clive, we felt we needed to give something back and get involved in any campaigns they were planning. So, when Norman asked us to join 15 other victims' families in an appeal to Tony Blair for greater public awareness of the impact of murder, we didn't hesitate. The letter was being sent to mark European Victims Week in February 2002 – an international initiative along the same lines as the ongoing work of VOCT.

In the petition, we appealed for the Government to consider funding trauma therapy for victims of homicidal crime through the criminal justice process and eradicate secondary victimisation. We also suggested appointing a Minister for Victims to back their interests and adopt International Victims Best Practices as recommended in the 1998 United Nations Handbook.

To maximise the publicity, we all agreed to meet and be photographed for an article about our appeal in the *News of the World*. The picture that appeared in the paper has to be one of the most powerful and painful images ever published because, for the first time, people were able to see the faces of some of us who, as the paper described, had 'endured the unendurable'. By signing the letter to Tony Blair, we were desperately hoping that our collective grief would make the powers-that-be sit up and take notice and make sure other parents didn't have to suffer the same loss in isolation.

It was an emotional but wonderful experience to meet so many other families who knew what we were going through. They were ordinary people like us who were trying to live lives that had been changed for ever and, yet, by sharing our stories, had still, somehow, found the courage to try and make a difference for others.

In many ways, it made Ray and me start counting our blessings and helped us to see that there were others who were far worse off than us.

There were 20 of us in the photograph, including Norman, Clive, Ray and me. I sat next to Denise Fergus, whose two-year-old son, Jamie Bulger, was killed in February 1993 by Robert Thompson and Jon Venables after they abducted him from a Bootle shopping centre in Merseyside. Next to her was Sara Payne. Her eight-year-old daughter was murdered by the paedophile Roy Whiting in July 2000 after he abducted her while she was playing in a field near her grandparents' home in Kingston Gorse, West Sussex.

We were surrounded by stories of unimaginable pain and amazing bravery as we sat for that photo: Frances Hogg's 27-year-old daughter Andrea Dykes was killed in the 1999 London Soho bomb attack on the Admiral Duncan pub;

Linda Tiltman's 16-year-old daughter Claire was stabbed to death as she walked home from school in Greenhithe, Kent, in January 1993; Janet MacKensie was the sister of 42-year-old Liz Sherlock, who was killed at London's Euston Station in 2001 as she chased two bag thieves; Barbara Hickmott's 19-year-old daughter Heidi was shot by her ex-boyfriend on the steps of her family home in Tenterden, Kent, in 1997; Georgina Wood and Danielle Rising were the mum and sister of Ricky Rising, who was just 19 when he was shot in the back in an East London pub in June 2000; Margaret and Brian Goodman's son Glenn, a 37-year-old special constable, was shot dead on a vehicle check in Tadcaster, North Yorkshire; Gaynor Tregembo's 20-year-old daughter Joanne was tortured to death by her ex-boyfriend in Swansea, South Wales; Charlie Ming's daughter, Julie Hogg, was only 23 when she was strangled in Stockton-on-Tees in 1989; Josie Russell's dad Shaun lost his wife Lin and younger daughter Megan when they were killed as they walked in a field in Chillenden, Kent, in 1996; and Alan West was the stepdad of Lesley Ann Downey, who was ten when she was killed after being stripped, tortured and sexually assaulted by Moors Murderers Myra Hindley and Ian Brady in 1964.

The sense of shared grief and the deep sadness of lives cruelly taken from us was heartbreaking. We'd all paid the price for the same mindless violence and it was almost unbearable to hear the stories behind the headlines, and to feel the impact of those murders that, like Lee's, had affected so many people who loved and missed them.

Many of the people we met that day made us realise that

the long-term effects of trauma lasted for years. Families had to be treated for depression, they'd lost their businesses and homes because they were unable to work or organise their finances and their relationships and marriages had suffered. And the lack of care or consideration for victims' families was extraordinary. Barbara Hickmott, who had cradled her dying daughter in her arms on her own front doorstep, had been offered a house backing on to the home of the killer's family when she asked the council if she could be rehoused; the families of Ricky Rising's killers had put up posters campaigning for their release in the cemetery where Ricky was buried; and Denise Fergus and Sara Payne both told me how their marriages had ended because they had found it impossible to cope with their loss.

Like Ray and me, they'd initially turned to drink to try to numb the pain, but both agreed that it only made you feel worse. Sara felt that victims had been neglected for years. 'You come to the end of a court case and you come to a dead end,' she said. 'That's just when a lot of families are only just beginning to pick themselves up.'

There were so many heart-rending stories to try and take in that day but one that I really felt I needed to lend my support to was the campaign by Julie Hogg's mum and dad Ann and Charlie Ming to repeal the ancient law of double jeopardy. Now, of course, we all know that Julie's killer Billy Dunlop is serving life after becoming the first person to be charged twice with the same offence after the 800-year-old double jeopardy laws were changed. The case made legal history in 2006 when Dunlop, 43, pleaded guilty to murder at the Old Bailey and marked the end of a 15-year battle by the Mings to have the law changed.

I don't think anyone will ever appreciate what Ann and Charlie went through, let alone the courage and determination that they found to keep fighting for justice. Julie's disappearance in November 1989 was initially treated as a missing person inquiry until Ann found her decomposing and partially mutilated body beneath the bath in her home. Police arrested Dunlop after his hair and semen were found on the body but, despite bragging about the murder in local pubs, admitting guilt to a prison officer and confessing to the crime in court ten years later, he never served time for Julie's murder because a jury failed to convict him.

Six months before I met Ann, Dunlop had instead begun a six-year sentence for the lesser charge of perjury. The double jeopardy law that was obviously still in force at the time meant he couldn't be tried for murder twice – even if he'd confessed to it in the dock. I told Ann I'd write to everyone on her list and mine to join her campaign. Thank God, she and Charlie got justice for their beautiful daughter in the end.

Michelle didn't come with us to the VOCT photo-shoot but wrote a heartfelt letter to Tony Blair asking him to make sure he read and acted on the charity's appeal. She wrote:

> *Dear Mr Blair,*
> *I am writing this letter to you today in the hope that you will actually read it and not just file it with all the others you get but actually take what I am saying into your heart and help families like mine.*

My brother was Lee Harvey, murdered by Tracie Andrews in December 1996. I don't want to bore you with the details. I just want you to realise that there is NO HELP for victims of crime.

We need a minister for victims of crime who can be there to help people like us and the many thousands of families who this is going to happen to over the coming years.

Last week, my parents met up with many families who have had children or family members murdered. Some of them have not even hit the headlines because of the way in which murder is an everyday event, because of the way you and governments before you have failed mankind.

The meeting was to try and get support and help and to make people aware that the victims of crime are not given a second thought while the murderers and perpetrators of these horrific crimes are given all the support in the world. God forbid that their needs aren't catered for!

All we are asking for is a minister to be instated for victims' needs, the Government to fund the Victims of Crime Trust so that better research can be done to help people, who through no fault of their own have been thrown into devastation and their lives torn apart because of these scumbags who are treated like royalty.

Do something about it. Stand up for the people who deserve it, instead of making sure the evil are catered for.

I have lost my business, and almost the will to live at times, so have thousands of other people affected by this horrific crime. All I have been offered is Prozac and told I should be over it by now.

It is not good enough, it's too late to help me and my family but I want to help other families! Please help us!

I will give my time and help others. Will you?

Yours sincerely,
M Harvey-Gill

Norman sent us all a copy of the letter he received from one of Tony Blair's senior policy advisers a month later in response to the one we'd all signed. It did recognise there was a lot more to be done for victim's families but, typically, made more of what the Government had done in the previous four years. And, really, it told us what most of us already knew – there had been more grants to Victim Support, increased criminal injuries compensation, the introduction of victim personal statements, a witness-support court service and the implementation of the Criminal Justice and Court Services Act to ensure greater Probation Service consultation.

The role of a Minister for Victims was, said the adviser, already being filled by the Home Office Minister Keith Bradley, but there were plans to widen the response to the needs of victims with a victims' commissioner. The response to our suggestion to adopt the United Nations' practice policy was lukewarm, to say the least: 'It is generally recognised that the support and services available in this country exceed what is available in most other jurisdictions, although others may do certain things better.'

And the old chestnut of funding? Until we improved the business plan that the Trust had already sent to Charles Clarke two years earlier, then, well, no decision could be made.

'We'll just have to keep shaking our collection tins and raising our own funds until then,' I told Norman.

20

Playing the Victim

A week later, we opened another letter, this time from Tony Hassall to our MP Julie Kirkbride, which said Tracie *had* given an inmate the kiss of life. The only thing the *Sun* had got wrong was the timing. It had happened during the previous year.

Tracie had received a routine thank-you letter but no official commendation. More importantly, for us, it wouldn't affect her sentence or entitle her to an early release. As a further token gesture, Mr Hassall said he'd met with the police to find out if anything could be done under the Data Protection Act to stop prison informants, officers, inmates and visitors supplying media stories.

It proved to be one of the most laughable suggestions we'd heard since Tracie's conviction because, two months later, a local newspaper reporter phoned at 7.30am to ask if we'd seen the *Daily Mail*. No one had bothered to tell us that Tracie had given an exclusive interview to reporters from the paper who had visited her in prison. To add insult to injury, the two-page interview had been published on the same day that a part-dramatised account of Lee's murder was televised in a *Real Life* Carlton production entitled *Blood on her Hands*.

It wasn't something we'd wanted to get involved with but, after the fight we'd had to stop the screening of the female murderers programme, we decided it was a case of 'if you can't beat 'em, join 'em'. And, because we were told the barristers from both sides and Tracie's mum Irene had agreed to be interviewed, we felt we couldn't ignore an opportunity to give a family perspective on Lee's death. It was on that basis that Michelle and I agreed to be interviewed for the programme.

I'm sure any victim's family faced with so many unauthorised and speculative reports about the aftermath of a high-profile murder investigation will know how frustrating it is not to have a voice. The publicity rarely ends once you've said your piece at a press conference and no one can ever prepare you for the emotional trauma that inevitably accompanies media calls asking for your reaction to the kind of stories we've had to put up with reading about Tracie. We decided that, if we were involved with the project from the beginning, then we'd be spared any nasty surprises when it was eventually broadcast.

You never know whether you're making the right decision but at least you feel there's an element of being in control and redressing any potential hurtful remarks made by other parties. We've learned the hard way that damage limitation is sometimes all that's left and is, more often than not, the only way to get your message across.

That said, I don't think we have ever felt as humiliated and upset as we did when we read Tracie's shameful testimony in the *Daily Mail* that day. Under the noses of Governors and prison officers, two reporters had visited her on several occasions to let her give a damning account of why she'd killed Lee. And, appallingly, why Tracie felt he was as much to blame for his death as she was.

'I've come to terms with what has happened and can accept that there's blame on both sides,' she said. 'Yes, I murdered Lee but he should take some of the responsibility. People saw him as an angel. I know he isn't here to defend himself now. But there were two sides to Lee. He was Jekyll and Hyde and, when he was awful to me, he made my life hell.

'I shouldn't be here. I'm stressed. I've had a terrible time lately. I've been on a roller-coaster of emotions and I've lost a stone in weight. Lee could be loving, caring and very charming. That was the side to him that I clung to. He worshipped me at the beginning. He loved the way I dressed and the way I behaved. But after a while he began to knock me off my pedestal and started chipping away at my self-esteem that was already so shaky. He also became obsessively jealous and violent towards me. For example, he used to plunge all my make-up in hot water to stop me wearing it, smash bottles of perfume and throw away one half of a set of high heels to stop me going out.

'Then he became violent and would hit me. I turned up at work with black eyes a couple of times. I would wear my hair down trying to cover them up. Once, when he was really angry over something, he bashed my head against a wall, tried to strangle me and almost choked me with a snooker cue.'

Once again, her description of what happened on the night of Lee's death was at total odds with the lies she'd told in court. She could recall her own graphic detail about killing Lee but couldn't remember what they'd argued about in the Marlbrook pub beforehand. The row, she claimed, had started because she talked to a bouncer as they left the pub. 'This set Lee off into a bad mood,' she said. We got into the car and he unleashed a torrent of abuse. "You're ugly," he screamed at me.'

She said, when the row intensified, she'd ordered Lee to stop the car. 'All I wanted to do was get away.' She said she got out when Lee had stopped and sped off and had then refused to get back in when he came back for her. When he came back a second time, she got in and they then missed their turning and drove up Cooper's Hill. She then said she got out of the car in a fury and sat crying on a nearby wall.

'Then I went and leaned against the back of the car. If only Lee had stayed in the car and not followed me. The next thing I knew, Lee yanked the back of my hair. He had a knife and was holding it up to my face – the knife he kept in his glove compartment. "I'm going to maim you," he screeched. "I'm going to maim you so that no one will fancy you." Lee had often threatened to do this but something inside me made me feel he was serious that night.

'I turned around to face him and kneed him in the groin. Lee collapsed on the floor and dropped the knife. He said,

"You bitch, I'm going to kill you." We fought and fell into a ditch. I saw the knife and ran and grabbed it. Lee got up and came over to me and hit me in the face. That's when I went into a frenzy.

'I just punched him... I just punched and punched. I wasn't even aware that I had the knife in my hand. I was just punching him. I'd lost control. Then I smelled the blood. It was awful, like the smell of metal. I was beside myself with panic. I didn't know what I was doing or saying. If I had wanted to kill Lee, I would not have done so outside a house.

'When Lee died, I died, too. I became a shell. The real Tracie had gone. I was extremely ill. I tried to kill myself three times.'

Tracie said she had invented the road-rage story because she was 'consumed with guilt'. 'I lied because I was terrified. I'd got myself into a black hole I suddenly couldn't get out of. Each day I was being carried along by fear. In the end, I almost began to believe the road-rage story was true.

'Your mind can play tricks on you like that and you begin to believe your own reality. I understand now I might have been convicted of the lesser charge of manslaughter if I had confessed at the time but I was in love with Lee, suffering from post-traumatic stress and I didn't want to blacken his name.

'During the trial, I felt as if I was in a goldfish bowl and being buried alive. Back then, I didn't even know what manslaughter meant. Looking back, I think if I had been kept in police custody instead of released on bail after my arrest, I would have been surrounded by other women and maybe it would have given me the courage to speak out. Lee's parents know what our relationship was like. It's just that their son is dead, so all the details of our relationship were buried in their minds.

'I'll be nearly 40 when I get out. I'm losing the best years of my life and that's really hard to deal with.'

For us, Tracie's interview was really hard to deal with. Another raft of sickening lies and insults to our precious son's memory. Every grubby detail served as a painful reminder of the evil intent with which she'd snuffed out Lee's life. She was right, too – we did, indeed, know what her relationship with Lee was like, just as she knew how hard we'd tried to convince him to cut her out of his life.

Throughout the interview, she hadn't shed a single tear for Lee. She hadn't shown any remorse or even bothered to apologise to us for her actions. It was an interview that showed how, even after five years in prison, Tracie remained as deluded and calculating as the day she killed Lee. She had had every opportunity to admit her guilt and yet she carried on lying because she didn't want to end up in jail. The fact that the interview mentioned how Tracie had written to charities asking them to send her clothes showed how she even believed she deserved public sympathy. All we could hope was that anyone reading the interview would dismiss her as the proven liar she will always be.

The dead, of course, can't speak, as I told Tony Hassall when I phoned him to find out why journalists had been allowed into Bullwood Hall to interview Tracie. She had known she was breaking the rules when she'd sent a visiting order to a reporter and yet no one had stopped the visit.

Mr Hassall told us that it would have been impossible to know whether someone visiting an inmate was a journalist. If officers discovered someone taking notes or using a tape recorder during a visit, the visit, he said, would be terminated. Well, no one had bothered to check if Tracie's reporter friend had settled down with a cup of tea and a tape hidden away, had they? No one had bothered that Tracie was still using every trick in the book to involve the press in her sordid fantasies about how she'd killed our son, and his level of culpability. Or that she was still getting away with murder of a different kind by fooling the Prison Service that she was a model inmate and still playing the victim.

I said we were sick of her lies and deceit and that we wanted to know she'd lose privileges for breaking the rules. If this kind of appalling behaviour was allowed to continue on a lifers' unit, what possible confidence could taxpayers have in the system?

'I'm not going to let this go away, Tony,' I told him. 'If I have to go to the top, the Prime Minister, MPs, the press... I want her moved from Bullwood Hall to somewhere where this kind of thing can never happen again. She might think she can make fools of the Home Office, but she's not going to do it to us.'

Tony Hassall told me that Tracie knew she'd blown it and that a move to another prison in Derbyshire, HMP Foston Hall, had already been arranged. By the end of that week, she'd be getting to know a new bunch of lifers. Hopefully, inmates who would have the benefit of having seen her treacherous, controlling way of dealing with life behind bars in the press reports we'd had to put up with. And who, this time, would damn well make sure she was soon put in her place and stripped of the top-dog lifer status that she'd obviously established at Bullwood Hall.

It was annoying to think that her family wouldn't have as far to go and visit her but it felt good to know that the bitch had unwittingly engineered a move which I hoped would make her fear the unknown.

The next thing I did was ring the *Daily Mail* to find out more about the freelance reporter who had interviewed Tracie. When I spoke to her, it wasn't a surprise to discover how shocked she'd been by Tracie's lack of emotion and remorse. Five years down the line, Tracie hadn't changed at all. She was still the same ice-cold, stone-faced, malevolent bitch we'd always known.

Next in my firing line was the Foston Hall Governor Paddy Scriven. On the phone, she told me that she would write to me once Tracie had been moved.

The letter arrived a week later:

> *Dear Mrs Harvey,*
> *I know I cannot begin to understand the pain that you and your family feel at the death of your son and how distressing the recent newspaper articles were. However, just as you wish the rules to be followed in respect of Tracie Andrews, I must follow them and I am not at liberty to discuss internal matters or individual prisoners with you – those are the rules.*

Ms Andrews has only just been received at this establishment and, as yet, we have limited dealings with her; nonetheless, we have a number of staff particularly experienced in dealing with life-sentenced prisoners and I hope we will be judged on our performance, not that of any others.

We are, of course, always open to the scrutiny of Parliament and our local MP is familiar with the establishment, so I am sure he will be able to give whatever assurances your local MP may need about the way the prison is run.

When Ms Andrews's parole dossier is eventually prepared, and that is a number of years off yet, you will be invited to make your views known. I hope until then you can attempt to move on, despite the unfortunate intervention of the press last week.

Yours sincerely,
Miss PG Scriven

There was, to use a line from Paddy Scriven, 'yet another unfortunate intervention of the press' just four weeks later. It was another example of how Tracie had spent her time at Bullwood Hall. This time, it wasn't a fashion show or working in the prison hair salon that had captured the *News of the World*'s attention, but details of how she'd conned a businessman into sending her parcels of designer clothing, sexy lingerie and, for good measure, a few grand in cash.

The story, headlined I WAS SENT A DEAD RAT AFTER JILTING EVIL TRACIE was horrendous. Steve Armstrong, a balding, middle-aged man from London, revealed how he'd started writing to Tracie in 1998 and, after six months, had gone on to visit her in prison. 'Her long blonde hair and low-cut top were very striking,' he told the paper. 'She was very flirty. It gave me a strange thrill. Afterwards, she asked for clothes. I went again two months later and we kissed for the first time in the visiting room. She was very complimentary about how I looked and made the first move.

'Within days, a list of clothes arrived, with instructions on where to get them. She wanted low-cut tops, G-strings and lacy bras.

'On our next visit, I touched her breasts and we fondled each other. It got steamy but there was no way we could take it further.'

In letters Tracie had sent to him, she'd told him, 'I'm used to being a dressy bird.' One said, 'The spoilsports here won't let me have that toy you wanted to send. They won't allow anything with batteries.' And, in another, she'd written, 'Book me in for an MOT. The full works. Check my spark plugs! Nudge, nudge!'

Armstrong, who said he'd forked out more than £5,000 for clothing and thousands more in cash for Tracie over three years, said Tracie had shown her true colours when he'd told her he wouldn't pay for any more gifts. 'She suddenly gave me a hard stare and made a veiled threat involving a friend who, she said, was a psychopath. I could see her eyes changed and a cold look came across her face as she said, "I want these clothes, Steve. Don't forget about my friend in Stafford."

'Then she just smiled and tried to hold my hand and make small talk but I wanted to go. I must admit I was scared because of the way she had turned. I got up, left and did not look back or say goodbye. She's sent me several letters but I haven't replied.

'Several months ago, she left a message on my home phone, again threatening me with the guy from Stafford. Then, after that, there was a big black rat on my mat. It had 'STEPHEN ARMSTRONG' written on a card fastened on an elastic band round its neck.

'Bullwood Hall was like a holiday camp. Tracie had her own video, television and computer. She got so fussy that, when I sent her some tapes, she sent them back. She got me to change them for CDs as she had a player in her room. She could decorate her room as she liked. One time, she wanted me to get her new curtains and a duvet cover.'

There was even a photograph of Tracie that she'd sent out with her shopping lists. She looked like she was on bloody holiday. Immaculately styled hair, dyed red, designer sunglasses, presumably courtesy of her businessman boyfriend, and a trademark plunging halter-neck top. How long, we wondered, would it take her to find another obliging pen-pal like Armstrong once she'd settled into similar five-star accommodation at Foston Hall?

21

Fighting Our Corner

In January 2003, we braced ourselves for yet another round in our endless battle against a system which, to us, seemed hell-bent on making Tracie's life as easy as possible. Our victim liaison officer Denise Astley sent us a letter in which, to our horror, she said she'd been notified that Tracie was being considered for escorted visits out of Foston Hall. We were aware that such visits were a possibility towards the end of her sentence, but not after serving just five-and-a-half years.

The thought that Danielle, who, at the age of 11, had just left primary school and faced the prospect of having to cope with another blaze of publicity about Tracie, was too much to bear. It was like having a bomb drop on us but, even as I sat reading the letter in floods of tears, I knew I couldn't just accept this appalling decision without making a stand. It was an insult to Lee's memory. It was bad enough not being able to go to our local shopping centre in case we ran the risk of bumping into Tracie's family, let alone cope with the idea that we might come face to face with Tracie herself.

The Prison Service was playing God with our lives and Tracie was sticking two fingers up at us and the system, no doubt having carried off yet another Oscar-winning performance to fool the Governor into believing she had changed.

Once again, I sent letters to the Home Office, the prison, the Probation Service and Julie Kirkbride, making it clear we'd do everything humanly possible to make sure Tracie stayed where she was.

It took less than a week to get a telephone call from Denise Astley saying she'd received an email from Tracie's probation officer with the news that it would be 'a good few years' before escorted visits were considered.

A month later, Julie had a letter from the Director General Martin Narey, which spelled out the Home Office's policy on the matter. It's a tip right from the top that I hope might help other victims' families if they suddenly find themselves facing the prospect of seeing their child's killer out shopping:

> Life-sentence prisoners are not eligible to apply for a visit to a town in the company of an officer until they are within four years of tariff expiry. No application is granted automatically and all are subject to a rigorous risk-assessment procedure. That risk assessment may include a report from the Probation

Service giving the views of the victim's family, if the family so wish.

As Ms Andrews' tariff does not expire until July 2011 and the Parole Board is not due to consider her case for the first time until July 2008, she will not become eligible for an escorted visit until July 2007.

Before any temporary release application is considered, the Probation Service is asked to ensure that the family of the victim has the opportunity to express any concerns they may have about such temporary release.

If necessary, specific conditions may be included in a temporary release licence to ensure that named individuals are not approached or contacted, or that the individual does not enter a clearly defined area.

Life-sentence prisoners are not eligible for temporary release on resettlement licence (a visit to the address at which they intend to reside on eventual release) until they are in an open prison. A lifer will move to an open prison only if the Parole Board recommends such a move and that recommendation is subsequently accepted by the Secretary of State.

Yours sincerely,
Martin Narey

Two months later, the front page of our local weekly newspaper, the *Sunday Mercury*, carried the headline SICK FANS IN TRACIE TAUNT.

Lee had always been a fan of Birmingham City Football

Club and we horrified to read that rival Aston Villa football fans were planning to goad Blues supporters by wearing blonde wigs and carrying flags with Tracie's name on them. The sick tribute was to have been staged at a match at Villa Park and was a follow-on from a previous derby match when Villa fans had chanted Tracie's name.

The *Mercury* had been tipped off by three separate supporters about the stunt who had told the paper that leaflets praising Tracie's killing of Lee had been printed by Villa fans in the build-up to the big match. Nearly 100 hooligans were also planning to smuggle long blonde wigs into the match and wear them to taunt Blues supporters, according to an email sent to the paper.

Chillingly, it said, 'Tracie is idolised by these hardcore fans as they see her killing a Blue Nose as an act of heroism.'

It was hard to imagine what kind of twisted minds could ever have dreamed up such an appalling stunt. Birmingham City had put up a £10,000 reward for information about Lee's killer in the week after he'd been murdered and, as I've mentioned earlier, his coffin was draped with a club flag.

Ironically, Ray and I had always worried about Lee going to matches in case anything happened to him. Ray stopped taking Lee to watch the team when Lee was about 12 or 13, after there was a riot at a Blues cup match against West Ham. He's never gone since but, as Lee got older, he started going with his mates.

Both football clubs had condemned the stunt with contemptuous statements to the paper and the police said they'd make sure it didn't go ahead.

In the end, the trouble that marred the game resulted from one of the Villa players being sent off after head-butting a Blues player. Mercifully, there were no blonde wigs or Tracie posters, although there were 40 arrests for fighting among a minority of supporters.

Since then, we've only been aware of one other attempt to use Tracie's name in sick Villa chants. The words appeared on a website chatroom but, because of the cowardly anonymity of the author, we couldn't do anything about it:

> *Tracie Andrews is our friend, she kills noses!*
> *Let her out to kill some more, kill some more, kill*
>   *some more*
> *Let her out to kill some more. Tracie Andrews!*
> *Tracie Tracie Tracie Andrews*
> *You're our hero 'cos you killed a Blues.*
> *You stabbed him in his head*
> *And now the bastard's dead.*
> *And he looks sweet, dead in the street.*
> *You are Villa and he was Blues.*

Two months later, there was a story in the *Sun* which, to us, again proved that prison officers at Bullwood Hall had underestimated Tracie's determination to do exactly what she wanted. This time, the ugly twist to details of her lesbian relationship with a prostitute serving life for murder was that Tracie had let Carla meet her evil new girlfriend.

Of course, we'd known intimate relationships between women were part and parcel of prison life and had suspected Tracie wouldn't take long to fulfil her sexual needs. Snogging and groping a bloke who looked old enough to be her dad obviously hadn't been quite as fulfilling as she'd told him. But the image of her 12-year-old daughter being introduced to Sharon Johnson, a woman who, according to the *Sun* story, had battered to death one of her elderly clients, was beyond contempt.

Johnson seemed to us like the perfect partner for Tracie, someone who she probably had far more in common with than any man she'd managed to snare. Like Tracie, Johnson had killed in cold blood. Her victim was a 69-year-old man who had died after being struck with a hammer at least 26 times. Like Tracie, Johnson knew what it was like to take an innocent life, to stand over a blood-spattered body and, consequently, to know how it felt to be told she would serve the best years of her life behind bars.

How happy they looked together in the photograph; Tracie with her red hair and Johnson with her beaded dreadlocks, side by side with another inmate whose arms were draped casually around their shoulders. Under the noses of warders, she and Tracie had had sex sessions in their neighbouring cells and in the prison's sick bay. And, thanks to a series of letters Tracie had written to an ex-inmate, the paper had described how they'd spent several hours alone together, including in bed, to celebrate their first anniversary as lovers.

'We went away for a little holiday,' Tracie had written. 'Miss S and I went over for a weekend on healthcare. We made it cosy, black bags up at the windows as curtains, pushed the beds together (kingsize!). IT WAS ALL GOOD!!!'

Johnson had even given her a pair of earrings for her

birthday. 'Before I opened the box they were in, I said, "I'm not marrying you. Ha, ha..."' added Tracie.

Ha, ha, indeed, Tracie Andrews. Would she still be laughing if she, for once, stopped thinking about her depraved sexual needs and thought, instead, of the emotional trauma she was heaping on to her daughter? These days, girls of 12 know far more about the facts of life than we ever did at the same age, so, even if Tracie had told Carla that Sharon Johnson was her mum's new best friend, did she honestly think the truth wouldn't come out? What hope of a normal life could Carla ever expect with a mother banged up for life for murder and making headlines with her newfound preference for lesbian sex?

That week, when I took Danielle with me to Lee's grave and watched her picking handfuls of daisies and buttercups to lay on some of the other graves that rarely seemed to have flowers on, I wondered what the hell life could throw at us next.

When she was younger, she had found a heart-shaped stone and painted the word 'DAD' on it with two kisses to place on Lee's grave. It's been there ever since, one of the most heart-breaking symbols of my beautiful grand-daughter's love for the father who made her world complete for a few precious years. It's a love that could stand the test of a thousand years. A beacon of pure, shining light in the darkness. Something that Tracie Andrews can never begin to understand, know or destroy. No matter how sickening and upsetting the stories in the press about her are, they won't break us. The only ones she can keep trying to destroy are her family.

In April 2004, I went to London to join the launch of a national fundraising petition for the Victims of Crime Trust. There were more than 60 relatives of murder victims, including Damilola Taylor's dad Richard, at the launch of a charity hotline aimed at attracting a million telephone donations. The idea was that the publicity would highlight the discrepancy between the £30,000 that was being spent annually on keeping a prisoner behind bars, and just £18.66 being spent on their victims and families. Norman Brennan had worked out the figure based on the annual Government grant to the charity Victim Support, divided by their number of clients.

It was wonderful to see so many familiar faces again, including Denise Fergus and Sara Payne and her husband Michael and their new baby daughter Ellie, who was then five months old. Sara told reporters that she hoped people would respond to the appeal because the impact of murder went on for generations and that Ellie might need someone to talk to when she was grown up.

Denise and I walked back to Euston Station together afterwards and had a few drinks while we were waiting for our trains. She's a lovely woman and said she knew only too well how hard it was to try and keep a marriage going after losing a child. You don't feel so lost and isolated when you can talk about the intimate side of your relationship with another woman who's been in the same boat and can reassure you that you're doing OK if you even manage to get through one day without crying.

We thought it had been too good to be true that the press hadn't picked up any more stories about Tracie but, two weeks after the VOCT petition launch, there was yet another story in the *Sun*. Tracie had found a new best friend at Foston Hall – Maxine Carr.

As part of her rehabilitation, Tracie had been coached by the Samaritans to help other inmates with their problems. Inside, prisoners who take on this informal role are called 'listeners', although quite how Tracie, who'd never listened to anyone in her life, was deemed to be suitable for such a job was anyone's guess. But she'd apparently been paired up with Maxine, who was in Foston Hall after being jailed for giving Soham school caretaker Ian Huntley an alibi after he'd killed Holly Wells and Jessica Chapman.

Typically, the story had been leaked by a 'source' who was quoted as saying it was a joke that two such notorious prisoners had been introduced to each other. 'Confiding in an evil bitch like Tracie must be so reassuring,' they'd told the paper.

With just nine days to go until her release at the time the story appeared, Maxine Carr had told everyone to call her Amanda, saying it was the name she expected to assume when she started life with a new identity. There were photographs of inmates at Foston Hall holding up banners outside their windows which said 'Burn the bitch on the stake. She's pure evil...' and 'Shoot her on the 17th' which was the day Carr was due to be released.

The thought of her pouring out her heart to someone as twisted as Tracie beggared belief but, with a track record like hers, I figured they probably had more in common than any of the other 'friends' Tracie had found.

Thankfully, the story appeared the day before Ray,

Michelle, Steve and I flew out to Palma Nova for a week's holiday with Danielle, Paige and Jordan. It meant that when reporters started phoning to ask for our reaction, as they always did when a story about Tracie appeared, we were long gone.

22

Brief Encounter

Palma Nova was a fantastic break, a chance for all of us to spend some quality time together, swimming, shopping and making the most of the sunshine. A holiday with children, as any grandparent knows, is always a happy time but Ray and I came back feeling so exhausted that we decided to book another two weeks in Spain on our own.

The day before we were due to go in July, I went to change the flowers on Lee's grave. It was a lovely sunny day and I felt good. As I got out of the car, I noticed a man in his mid-forties, dressed all in black, standing on the pathway. He was staring at me but, at first, I thought he was just visiting a grave and ignored him. I was still doing the flowers when Michelle, Steve, Paige and Jordan pulled up alongside my car. They'd come to see the new picture of Lee that I'd had replaced on his grave because the old one had faded. They didn't stay long because they were all going shopping so I waved them off and carried on tidying the grave.

Lost in thought, I jumped when a shadow cut across the sunlight behind me and I turned round to see the man in black. 'Hello,' he said. 'Are you Lee's mum?' He beamed and started chatting when I introduced myself. 'I've been coming up here for the last seven years in the hope of meeting you,' he said.

I couldn't help feeling a bit uneasy at the way he was still staring at me but didn't want to appear rude. 'Were you a friend of Lee's?' I asked him.

'Yes, I met him in Baker's nightclub. I can't believe what that bitch did to him.'

It struck me as odd that a man so much older than Lee would be a friend from the nightclub.

'You look really well, Maureen,' he continued. 'Have you been away somewhere?'

I told him that Ray and I had been on holiday with the children and were looking forward to having a break on our own. 'Do you come here to see someone's grave?' I asked, starting to walk back to my car.

The man laughed. 'No, I come to see Lee but the person I've really always wanted to see was you. After Lee died, I went into every single hair salon in Alvechurch looking for you. One day, I actually plucked up the courage to go inside one and ask for you but the man who owned it said he thought you owned one in King's Heath.'

I did remember being told that a man had been looking for me in Alvechurch not long after Lee had died. I'd assumed it was another reporter who wanted a story from me.

The man was walking alongside me. 'Actually, I was only looking at a video of you a few days ago,' he said. 'I've got every newspaper cutting about the case and all the videos of the trial with you on. I'm glad you've had a new picture of Lee put on his gravestone. I thought the old one was looking a bit faded. I always know when you've put fresh flowers on. That's why I come up here most weekends in the hope of seeing you. I actually work in the flower business but I'm off at the moment because I had an accident.

'I can't believe my luck that I've finally found you. I expect Lee's death has really affected your marriage, hasn't it?'

I'd had enough of him; I just wanted to get in the car and leave. He was really starting to make me feel scared. 'Ray and I are very lucky that we have such a strong relationship,' I told him.

'So you wouldn't consider going out with me, then?' he asked.

I was shocked but tried to look composed. 'No, of course, not,' I told him. 'I'm happily married.'

He looked surprised by my answer. 'Please, I'd really like us to meet up. I live in the area... let me give you my number or you give me yours.'

I didn't want to show him I was scared when I reached the car. I thought, if I could try and laugh off his suggestions, he'd get the message and leave me alone.

'I don't think your wife would be very happy if she knew you went round asking women out,' I said.

'I haven't got a wife,' he laughed. 'Just a girlfriend... she lives in Leamington Spa and I only see her at the weekend. We have a pretty open relationship. She doesn't mind me

257

seeing other women. Will you go out with me? I don't smoke or drink and we don't even have to have sex if you don't want.'

I couldn't believe this was happening to me, in a bloody cemetery of all places. This was the one place where I'd always been able to come and spend an hour or so with Lee, sitting and thinking, to escape from the world. Now, this stranger, who seemed completely unaware of how frightened I was, had apparently been stalking me since Lee's death. I looked round, desperately hoping that I'd spot someone tending a grave or walking along a path. I had to get away.

There was an elderly lady sitting on a bench not far from the path at the other side of where I'd parked. Could I walk over to her and pretend she was a friend? I wondered. What if this guy suddenly turned nasty? What if he was carrying a weapon? I couldn't risk him turning on both of us.

I'd never felt so vulnerable as I did that day and thought that, if I could just keep him talking long enough to make him think I, and not he, was in control of the situation, he'd give up and leave.

'Well, I must be going,' I said, backing away from him. 'It's been nice meeting you.'

'I bet you can't guess my name, Maureen,' he said.

I told him I didn't like playing games and, no, I couldn't guess his name.

He told me his name but seemed completely unaware that I was trying to make my excuses and leave.

'Look, why don't you give me a ring when you get back from your holiday, I'd really love to take you out for a drink. If you won't give me your number, you can take mine.'

I could see lots of strips of paper in his wallet, all with his name and mobile number on, but, when I wouldn't take one and told him again that I was happily married, he grabbed my arm and forced his number into my hand. I decided that, if I just took the paper and left, he'd get the message. Thank God, it worked and he started walking away.

My heart was pounding as I leaned against my car door watching him go. He was still smiling as he turned round to look at me. I could hardly get my keys into the door I was in such a state but, when I realised I hadn't actually filled up the vase on Lee's grave with water, I ran over to a tap. The old lady was still sitting on the bench and had stopped reading her book to look at me, just as the man pulled up alongside me in his white van.

'Maureen, PLEASE,' he said, through the open window, 'I just want to take you out and talk to you. PLEASE RING ME.'

I shook my head. I'd had enough and felt braver knowing I was a lot closer to the old lady. 'No, thanks... please, can you just leave me alone?' I told him.

As he drove off, I threw the piece of paper in a nearby bin and went over to ask the pensioner if she'd heard him talking to me. She said she'd thought we were friends because she'd heard him tell me he'd been looking for me for seven years. 'I often come and sit in here near my husband's grave,' she explained. 'I love the peace and quiet. But that chap was here when I came about three hours ago, he was standing near your son's grave. I'd ring the police if I was you. You can count on me if you need a witness... and I'd get his number back out of the bin. The police will be interested to see it. They'll probably be able to trace him if he's telling the truth.'

I knew she was right. I went back and got the number and then rang Michelle and told her what had happened.

'Just get in the car, lock the doors and drive straight home, Mum,' she said anxiously. 'Ring the police and tell them you're being stalked.'

I rang Brian Russell, our liaison officer, as soon as I got in and explained what had happened.

'Well, we can't do him for stalking you for seven years if he's only just approached you now,' he told me. 'But I'll do some checks on him. Try not to worry... just go and enjoy your holiday.'

It was easier said than done. The thought that this man might try and approach me again kept going through my mind. Even though I'd told the police, there was no guarantee that they'd be able to do anything about him.

Ray and I tried to make the most of our time together but a few days into the holiday we got chatting to a man who was staying at the same resort with his wife.

'Do you know, your faces *are* familiar,' he said. 'Did you say you come from Birmingham?'

Ray and I looked at each other. It had happened before. We'd meet people who would start quizzing us about why we looked familiar to them. Sometimes, we'd immediately tell them who we were but at other times we were too upset to go through the whole story and just hoped they'd drop the subject.

The man we met in Spain was determined to try and place us. 'Something terrible happened in Alvechurch about six years ago, didn't it?' he persisted. 'But I can't for the life of me think what it was. It'll come to me eventually. I just know I've seen you two before.'

Ray wanted to put him and his wife out of their misery but I didn't want everyone in the resort coming up to us and telling us how sorry they were. In the end, it was like a farce. No matter how we tried to steer the conversation away from his guessing game or even tried to avoid sitting with the couple, the husband was like a dog with a bloody bone.

'We're not going to get any peace at this rate, Maureen,' Ray said crossly one evening as we were going into the bar and spotted them waving at us. When Ray explained that Lee had been murdered, the look on both their faces was priceless.

'God, we're so sorry,' the man said, looking uncomfortably at his wife. She looked just as embarrassed and didn't know what to say to us.

'Don't worry,' Ray said kindly. 'It happens a lot. That's why we've come on holiday... to get away from people reminding us.'

It was upsetting because Ray and I ended up comforting the couple, who were struggling to cope with their embarrassment, when all we felt like doing was sitting there and having a good cry.

It was almost a relief to get home, two weeks later. It was Paige's birthday and Michelle and Steve picked us up from the airport, stopping off on the way home to visit the cemetery. I hadn't heard anything from the police about the strange man I had seen there and felt nervous as we all got out of the car. 'What if he's here again?' I asked Ray, slipping my arm through his.

Ray laughed. 'Listen, Maureen, I hope he is here because it'll be the last cemetery visit he ever does.'

After going to see my mum's grave, we got to Lee's and Ray noticed what he thought was a bit of rubbish under Danielle's heart-shaped stone. None of us could believe it when he opened the slip of paper and saw it was identical to the one the man had given me with his name and mobile number on.

When I phoned the police again, they said they'd come round and take a statement from me. Now that he'd been back to the cemetery looking for me, they could do something. This time, after tracing him, they went round to his home and found he'd collected all the newspaper cuttings about Tracie's trial. There were tapes and videos about the news coverage and, chillingly, pictures of me which he'd cut out of the papers and stuck on his walls. He admitted that he'd spent seven years trying to contact me and approach me in the cemetery, but said he was sorry and hadn't meant any harm. He was cautioned for his behaviour and told in no uncertain terms that, if he ever came anywhere near me again, he would face harassment charges.

I felt sick to think a complete stranger could have become so obsessed with me because of Lee's death. It would have been far easier to understand if it had been about Tracie, but far too close to home for my liking. The police told me never to go to Lee's grave alone after that. I cried... more out of frustration and anger than fear of the unknown. Going to see Lee was all I had and it seemed so unfair that even that had been violated. Unfair, cruel, sickening... but I've always taken their advice.

I rang Ken and Toni Cameron to tell them what had happened. They were really upset but it was comforting to be able to share it with people who knew how we all felt. They said they were going to visit Toni's brother Bill, who lives near us, and called in for afternoon tea. Michelle and Steve and the children came round and we had a wonderful time, sharing stories and laughing. It's times like that which really help you get through the worst of the bad times. And we did it all over again the next weekend when we went to stay with them.

It was just what the doctor ordered. Toni cooked us some lovely meals, the children played on the beach near their home and took the dogs for long walks. We've never stopped counting our blessings and thanking God to have found such a true friendship in our sorrow.

23

Costa del Foston

There was another shock in store for us in October 2004 when we discovered Tracie's solicitor Tim Robinson had been convicted of fraud. The details had been made public for the first time that month after a judge lifted reporting restrictions after the final hearing in the case at Bristol Crown Court. It was reported in several papers that Robinson had been jailed for seven years in 2001 and released on parole in July 2004. Twenty-one ex-employees of his law firm were also convicted of fraud after a major police investigation that had started back in April 1993. It was estimated that up to 90 per cent of Robinson's firm's claims for Legal Aid were fraudulent with clerks exaggerating time spent with clients and billing for non-existent cases. Robinson had appealed against his conviction and then his sentence in October 2002 but had lost both appeals.

In May 2005, the *News of the World* printed yet another story. It was, for us, one of the worst articles we'd seen since Tracie's conviction. Not because of what she was getting up to, although that was bad enough, but because it served as a truly shocking indictment about the prison system and showed how lifers – those who have committed the most heinous crimes – are seemingly allowed to spend their sentences doing exactly as they please.

Under Foston Hall rules, she had been offering phone sex to a new pen-pal from inside the prison and, when he'd tipped off the paper, she obliged an undercover reporter by talking dirty. In the late-night call she'd received from the pen-pal, she'd allegedly told him, 'My name's Tantalising Tina and I can certainly tantalise your tackle. I've got a little blue vest top on, some light pyjama bottoms. That's it. No underwear.'

For the reporter, she'd played out a sex scene as Frisky Felicity. 'My hair's up... I have bronze nail polish on my toenails and a Rotary watch on my wrist. I'm going to take you for the ride of your life – hold back on those reins.'

In letters to both the pen-pal and the reporter, she'd described life at Foston Hall as 'like living in a big boarding school or Costa del Foston... You're never locked in your room. They only lock the front door. We're unsupervised, too. They do roll calls during the day but, apart from that, we're left alone. I'm in a separate flat in the hall itself. I even have my own bathroom – it's like being in a Travelodge. And I share a big lounge with the other girls, with a PlayStation, digital telly and a hi-fi.

'And there's none of that porridge and bread and water

stuff... We get curries, casseroles, pasta and fish... the menu's not too bad.'

She'd also talked about her lesbian affair, bragging about how much she'd enjoyed it. 'I'm glad I experienced it. One thing led to another in the bedroom. It was great – a bit weird at first – but it felt right. Every now and again, there might be a woman who I like the look of. I'm up for taking part in experiments. There are a lot of women in here who just do it for immediate gratification and just switch from one to another. They go all butch and cut their hair, but, I'm sorry, I'm not going to be attracted to a girl just because she looks like a man. I'm physically attracted to men mainly. And I do take care of my appearance. I shall never be saying, "Sorry, darlin', not tonight, I've got a headache."

'I'm a girlie girl. I like to dress up. I'm very feminine. I'm a bit like Julia Roberts in *Pretty Woman*. That's what I want – the fairytale. I'm waiting for a prince. I didn't realise how strong I was. I'm seldom down-hearted. I smile every day. I feel now that I have all the qualities to make my life a nicer place to live.'

It wasn't surprising to learn that she was still wielding the scissors in the prison hair salon but we were shocked to see her admitting that she even did the Governor's highlights and lowlights. Well, that's what she claimed, anyway.

The line that hurt us most was her reference to Lee's murder. It's a quote that we will never forget: 'There's no use crying over spilled milk,' she said.

Absolutely no use at all, Tracie Andrews, I thought, as I read her words over and over again with tears streaming down my face. Lee had meant nothing to her in life; why would he have meant any more to her in death?

I got a simple 'no comment' from the Deputy Governor at Foston Hall when I phoned the prison, so I wrote letters of protest to Tony Blair, the Home Secretary Charles Clarke, Paddy Scriven and the National Offender Management Service. The only time I came up for air was to blow my nose and wipe away the tears that blurred the words on my computer screen. I guessed the responses would be filled with the usual trite platitudes that we'd seen time and time again but, as with all the letters I've ever written, it's enough for me to know that they automatically go into a file marked 'Tracie Andrews'. When we reach the time for her to be eligible for parole, they'll still be gathering dust in various government offices, but the point is that they'll be there. The letters and the newspaper cuttings that have ripped out the hearts of everyone in our family will, hopefully, one day have some bearing on Tracie's parole hearing. The authorities who will finally assess Tracie's suitability for freedom will know that, even if they haven't been keeping an eye on what she's being doing in prison, then her victim's family most certainly has.

The letter that came back from Pat Baskerville at the National Offender Management Service did, at least, acknowledge our distress. Part of the letter read:

In a country like ours, with a free press, coverage of criminal cases during and after a trial cannot easily be prevented.

Regrettably, it is the case that, while they persist,

such stories continue to impose a burden on victims and their families. While the Home Office and its agencies do not themselves comment on individual cases, we recognise that this does not prevent reports being published about individual offenders, which may or may not be accurate, and which can cause considerable upset.

I can assure you that basic conditions in prisons are far from luxurious. As an example, the cost of feeding a prisoner averages less than £2 a day. Certain facilities are provided as a matter of decency. These include the means to contact friends and family, who can be important factors in rehabilitation. All prisoners are able to make telephone calls at their own expense. While this facility is generally used to keep in touch with family and friends, it is a matter for individuals who they choose to call.

However, prisoners can be prevented from calling certain numbers, including those of any victims, if particular concerns are raised.

Paddy Scriven's letter laid the blame with the *News of the World*:

I am unable to comment on individual prisoners, but you may wish to note that the article was published in the News of the World, *which is not best known for accurate reporting.*

Foston Hall, like all prisons, is run in accordance with prison rules and while every prison sentence is in itself a deterrent, the duty of the Service is also to address and correct offending behaviour. This is challenging both for staff and the prisoner. Few offences are single acts, all have complex components that have to be identified and dealt with. In the case of life-sentenced prisoners, release on parole is based on risk assessment and, if risk exists, release is not an option.

As far as how articles such as appeared in the News of the World *came to be published, the answer is very simple. This country has considerable press freedom. A great deal of money is made from newspapers and a sizeable section of the public prefer to be entertained rather than informed. Editors of many tabloid newspapers pay large sums to people who will provide a story that will increase sales, with little regard to its veracity or the very people it damages.*

From Eleanor Hodge at the Department of Culture, Media and Sport, the response was pretty much along the same lines:

The Government firmly believes that a press free from state intervention is fundamental to democracy and it would not, therefore, seek to interfere in any way in what a newspaper chooses to publish. This does not mean, however, that newspapers may publish just what they like; they sign up to a Code of Practice overseen by the Press Complaints Commission. The Code contains clauses about the need to avoid intrusion into grief or shock, but this does not restrict the right or the duty of newspapers to report.

It is an unfortunate fact that the nature of much news material is upsetting, and that those directly involved may find any report unwelcome. I am sure that you would understand that this cannot be a reason for not publishing stories.

However, if you see stories where you think material has been handled insensitively, then you should consider contacting the editor; it is important that newspapers be made aware when their readers are not happy with editorial decisions.

You may also be concerned about the source of the stories and, although journalists have a moral obligation to protect confidential ones, you will be interested to know that newspapers may not make payment for stories to convicted or confessed criminals or their associates, unless they can demonstrate that the story was in the public interest and there was no other way to obtain it.

If the five letters that appeared in the *News of the World*'s letters column the week after the phone-sex article appeared were anything to go by, then at least we knew public opinion was on our side. Each one of the correspondents felt Tracie's behaviour was a disgrace and, like us, they'd believed that prison was meant to be a deterrent to other prisoners.

Five months later, the *People* published a story about Tracie's new lesbian affair with a young inmate at Foston

Hall. Yet another source reckoned the two of them had been caught on two occasions doing God only knows what together but, again, Tracie had escaped any sanctions. More tears, more letters for the file and always the despair of knowing that, in Tracie's case, the punishment she received can never ever fit the crime.

We knew she'd never do her time quietly and that our lives will always be inextricably linked with hers, but I don't think any of us ever believed we'd spend so much time and energy fighting for our rights as victims in the face of the ones she continues to enjoy as the perpetrator.

The media has always been there for us when we've needed it and I'd like to believe it always will be so. As a family, our argument has never been against the newspapers for printing stories about Tracie's life in prison. I'm sure there'll be more to come before she gets out. The question I will continue to level at the justice system which fails to look after the interests of victims and their families is why she has been given the access to document her sentence with anyone she chooses to write to or allow to visit her. We live in a society which is now so closely scrutinised and controlled by government agencies and yet criminals with no regard for the consequences of their actions seem to be pandered to in the name of rehabilitation.

The most recent letters I've received from the Home Office, while writing this book, carry a slogan which is printed at the bottom of the stationery. It says 'Building a safe, just and tolerant society'. I wonder if the people who were presumably paid to come up with this catchy mission statement on the Government's behalf have any real understanding of what it's like to be a victim of crime. Ordinary families like mine wake up, just as we did, in the middle of the night and suddenly find their lives are never going to be the same again because of some mindless thug. Prisoners get released but the families whose lives they've ruined have to carry on serving a life sentence of sorrow and pain.

Tracie's 14-year life tariff expires in July 2011 and we've been assured by the Home Office that she will have to serve her term in full before the Independent Parole Board will consider her suitability for release on life licence. In December 2003, sections 269–277 of the Criminal Justice Act 2003 came into force and transferred the power to set and reset tariffs for mandatory life-sentence prisoners to the judiciary. Within the Act, there's a provision allowing prisoners like Tracie, who have unexpired tariffs set by the Secretary of State, to apply to the High Court to have their tariff reviewed and possibly reduced. As I write, Tracie hasn't made such an application, but there's no deadline for her to do so.

If she does apply, we'll be notified by the victim liaison office and we'll be allowed to submit a statement which would be seen by the judge who considers the case. It helps that her tariff was set in line with recommendations made by the trial judge and the Lord Chief Justice following the trial, but there are no guarantees that she won't get a reduction. According to the most recent Parole Board figures, the number of lifers let out early on licence has more than doubled in five years. In 2005, 140 life-sentence offenders had to be sent back to jail, 87 because they had committed further offences. Five years ago, there were only 26 returners, but there are those who feel that the rise is due to increasing pressure to free prisoners to ease the jail-overcrowding crisis. The number of lifers released early on licence has soared from 129 in 2000 to 307 in 2005, and there are 1,495 lifers being monitored in the community.

When Labour came to power, there were fewer than 5,000 parole requests and barely one-third of these were granted. But in 2005, the Parole Board considered 7,528 requests and granted 3,718. When you consider that lifers who are meant to be locked up for a long time are being released at the earliest opportunity, it does seem that the Government's obsession with keeping people out of prison is putting the public at greater risk. Confidence in the criminal justice system must be undermined if someone can be sentenced to life and then be released in three to four years.

24

Remembering Lee

W hen I look back at so many letters, newspaper cuttings and the videos of the news bulletins about the case, it sometimes feels as if I'm looking at someone else's family. It's still incredible to remember how we survived the early days after Lee's death. You think to yourself, Did we really get through all that?

In those early days, you just go through the motions. You can't make plans for the next day, let alone the next week. You don't want to know that other people are getting on with their lives. You don't want to feel resentment and bitterness because their lives haven't changed. You don't want to keep on fighting against such destructive emotions, but you do.

When I went to Ray's brother's funeral in September, I couldn't say the Lord's Prayer. It will always be a prayer that stops me in my tracks because of the line about forgiving our trespassers who trespass against us. My faith in God was always so comforting before we lost Lee but, afterwards, prayers and trying to make sense of why he'd been taken from us seemed meaningless. I want my faith back, but I can't say the Lord's Prayer any more. I can't ever forgive Tracie Andrews for what she did to our family.

The barriers I've put up are never going to come down now. I'm suspicious of people's motives for wanting to know me; I don't want anyone to get close to me. And, every Sunday, Ray and I watch the clock in our sitting room, reliving the moment when Lee was killed. We can't help it. It's something we've just always done, consciously or subconsciously, since the night the police turned up at our front door. It's a case of 'now Lee and Tracie will be coming out of the Marlbrook... now they're driving towards Alvechurch... now she's getting out of the car... stabbing him... watching him take his last breath. Now he's dead.'

I can't drive down a narrow country lane without getting flashbacks of Lee's drive to his death. Even if I'm in the passenger seat, I panic. I feel like screaming; the sweat pours off me and I shake with panic. I have to plan my routes pretty carefully when I go out, just to make sure I don't end up having to stop the car and get out before I feel really ill.

Ray and I still expect Lee to walk through the door and, as strange as it must seem after all these years, we still can't believe he's gone. He was wonderful. Everyone who met him, even if it was only for a few minutes, took a shine to him. He just had this special aura about him which lit up any room he walked into. Good-looking, kind, no angel, but an easy-going lad who always looked out for others. If only there had been someone looking out for him the night Tracie ended his life.

We cherish every single memory of him.

Danielle, who's now 15, loves hearing all our stories about him growing up and looking at the photo albums with us. We still chuckle remembering how, when he started playschool, he couldn't wait to get there early so he could ride a scruffy old red-and-blue bicycle. He had a brand-new one at home that we'd bought him, but the one at playschool was his favourite. He was thrilled when we asked the teachers if we could swap the bikes and bring the battered old one home with us. I don't think I'll ever forget the looks on the children's faces when I turned up with Lee one morning and handed over his gleaming new bicycle to the teacher.

He was only four years old when someone accidentally left a door open at the playschool and Lee decided to make his escape and catch a bus. I still shudder to think what could have happened to him if he hadn't been spotted by one of the hairdressing clients on the number 4 bus that day. He'd already sat in a seat quite happily and done two full round trips before she got on, recognised him and brought him safely back to me at the salon.

When she asked where I was, he told her, 'I'm on my own today. I'm going to be a bus driver when I grow up.'

When he was six, I managed to get a final appointment at the dentist because he had a really bad toothache but, because it was too late to give him an anaesthetic, he bravely announced he'd have his tooth out without any drugs. He just sat in the chair, good as gold, and never cried.

At school, he was always popular and got good grades for his work. He loved swimming, camping and outdoor activities and joined the Air Cadets as soon as he was old enough. I have a lovely picture of him looking so smart and handsome in his uniform, taken on the day he flew a light aircraft. Some of the friends he made there were at his funeral.

Lee's love of sport was something that started at school and went on until he died. He and Ray were regulars at the local golf club; he won trophies in snooker tournaments and played cricket for his works team.

On special anniversaries like 1 December and his birthday on 20 September, I always go to St Martin's Church in the Birmingham Bullring to light candles for him. I always take Danielle and my friend Joyce. The two of them make me laugh with the number of candles they light for friends. It's a wonder we haven't needed a fire extinguisher.

At Christmas time, there's a big tree in the church where you can hang little paper leaves with a message on to a loved one and they're read out at different services. Lee loved Christmas more than any other time of year. He always decorated our tree at home with Danielle, knowing that I'd be waiting for the two of them to disappear into another room before discreetly taking five or six baubles and stars off one branch. He knew what I was like. Typical me. It had to be perfect.

But now I'd give anything to see him in our sitting room, putting tinsel on his head to make Danielle laugh and letting her pile all the decorations on to three or four branches.

We didn't put the tree up for five years after Lee died. It was too upsetting. But, when Danielle asked us why we didn't get it out any more, I knew it was time to make an effort for her, Paige and Jordan. You can't stop the world turning. Even when your heart's breaking.

As a family, we're a lot stronger now because we've learned to help each other through the dark days. When one of us feels down, the others do their best to stay up. It's not easy, because, instead of it being the four of us, now it's just the three of us... but we'll never give up fighting and living our lives as best we can.

Having Danielle gives us more hope and happiness than we could have ever imagined. She reminds us so much of her dad. Like all teenagers, there are times when she struggles to make sense of what happened and cries because she misses him so much. She knows she's loved and, with our continuing support, there's no reason why she won't grow up and find the same happiness she knew when Lee was alive.

Danielle is one of the reasons I've written this book, and to give a sense of hope and peace to others who have travelled or who have yet to travel the same path. It's also a personal tribute to Lee's memory. My way of marking the last ten years with an honest account of what our lives were like before he died and the journey we've taken since.

Of course, we haven't heard the last of Tracie. There'll be more stories, more photographs and, inevitably, a lot more of her lies to deal with. She'll always be in my nightmares until I take my last breath. But I hope I'll always be in hers.

For now, all we can do is wait, watch and pray that she

stays where she is. We already know she's hoping to change her identity before she's released and has apparently changed her name by deed poll to Tia Carter. The 'T' is from Tracie, 'I' comes from Irene, her mum's name, and the 'A' is from Andrews. The surname is courtesy of her stepdad Alan. Laughably, she's told other inmates at Foston Hall that the name means 'princess' in Greek and that she thinks it's cute.

'Cute' is the last word anyone could ever call Tracie. But then there's hardly likely to be a Greek translation of the name 'Evil Conniving Bitch'.

A leopard never changes its spots. Tracie, no matter whom she tries to fool or how hard she tries to reinvent herself, will always be pure evil.